Routledge Revivals

William Shakespeare: The Anatomy of an Enigma

First published in 1990, the aim of this book is to reveal the William Shakespeare whose life has been obscured by centuries of literary mythology. It unravels a series of strands in order to understand the man and the major influences which shaped his life and writing. The first part advances the thesis that his relationship with his father directly influenced the character of Falstaff — helping to not only explain key events in his father's life but also critical events in his own biography. This thesis not only illuminates the Falstaff plays but also a number of other works such as Hamlet. The second part focuses on Shakespeare's own life, and includes much original research particularly on the tradition that he was a poacher of deer, discussing the influence this incident had on his later life and writings. In addition, a sociological approach has been used which illuminates a number of key areas, including questioning the view his background was narrow and provincial — which has often been used to dispute his authorship of plays of such cosmopolitan appeal.

William Shakespeare

The Anatomy of an Enigma

Peter Razzell

Routledge
Taylor & Francis Group

First published in 1990
by Caliban Books

This edition first published in 2017 by Routledge
2 Park Square, Milton Park, Abingdon, Oxon, OX14 4RN
and by Routledge
711 Third Avenue, New York, NY 10017

Routledge is an imprint of the Taylor & Francis Group, an informa business

Publisher's Note
The publisher has gone to great lengths to ensure the quality of this reprint but points out that some imperfections in the original copies may be apparent.

Disclaimer
The publisher has made every effort to trace copyright holders and welcomes correspondence from those they have been unable to contact.

A Library of Congress record exists under LC control number: 91188258

ISBN 13: 978-1-138-22071-3 (hbk)
ISBN 13: 978-1-315-41209-2 (ebk)
ISBN 13: 978-1-138-22073-7 (pbk)

Preface to the New Edition

Since the publication of the original edition of this book, no significant new biographical information on Shakespeare has become available, except for research by Jayne Archer and colleagues published in 2014. In their book on food and the literary imagination, they discussed Shakespeare's hoarding of grain and his other business activities, summarized as follows:

> During a period of dearth… for those with ready cash, it was a time of opportunity. William Shakespeare, a gifted recycler of plots, saw his chance. … over a 15-year period, Shakespeare purchased food-producing land and stored grain, malt and barley for resale (most likely at inflated prices) to neighbours and local tradesmen. In February 1598 he was prosecuted for holding 80 bushels of malt or corn during a period of shortage – an act similar to the charge leveled against the patricians in *Coriolanus*, who keep 'their storehouses crammed with grain' while allowing the citizens to 'famish'. He pursued those who could not (or would not) pay him in full for these staples and used the profits to further his own money-lending activities … Combining legal and illegal activities – and grain hoarding during a period of shortage was regarded with particular opprobrium – Shakespeare was able to retire in 1613, at the age of 49, as one of the largest property owners in his own town.[1]

A lecture by Jayne Archer at the *Telegraph Hay Festival* on the 23 May 2013, presented the above findings, which attracted world-wide media attention, much of it of a sensational nature.[2] According to the *Sunday Times,* Dr Archer stated that 'there was another side to Shakespeare besides the brilliant playwright – as a ruthless businessman who did all he could to avoid taxes, maximize profits at others' expense and exploit the vulnerable – while writing plays about their plight to entertain them.'[3]

---

[1] Jayne Elisabeth Archer, Richard Marggraf Turley and Howard Thomas, *Food and the Literary Imagination* (Palgrave Macmillan, 2014), pp. 82, 83.
[2] There were for example the following publications: 'Shakespeare was tax-evading food hoarder', *The Telegraph,* 13 March 2013; 'Study sheds light on Bard as a food hoarder', BBC News, 1 April 2013; 'Shakespeare was a ruthless profiteer and tax dodger' *Los Angeles Times*, 1 April 2013; 'Bad Bard? Shakespeare profited from famine by hoarding grains.' *USA Today*, 2 April 2013; 'New study finds that Shakespeare was tax-evading, grain-hoarding asshole', AV Club Newswire, 1 April 2013; 'Knowing Shakespeare fiddled his taxes tells us nothing', *Independent*, 3 April 2013.
[3] *Sunday Times*, 31 March 2013.

While it is true that Shakespeare did hoard grain in 1598 – as discussed later in this book – he did so in the company of virtually all of the wealthy men living in and around Stratford at the time. This included all four local magistrates who were meant to enforce the legislation against the forestalling and hoarding of grain.[4] This activity was commonplace among the wealthy, including Shakespeare's father, who had a long history of money lending and illegal speculation in a range of commodities, including grain and other foodstuffs.

In 1588, John Shakespeare claimed in a legal dispute that by losing twenty pounds, he had 'totally lost and failed to acquire the whole gain, advantage and profit which he by buying and bargaining with the aforesaid twenty pounds have had acquired to the loss of thirty pounds.'[5] He had included his son William in this legal submission, and the involvement of Shakespeare in his father's trading activities is confirmed by his first biographer, Nicholas Rowe:

> His Father, who was a considerable Dealer in Wool … could give him no better Education than his own Employment. He had bred him, 'tis true, for some time at a Free-School, where 'tis probable he acquir'd the Little Latin he was Master of: But the narrowness of his Circumstances, and the want of his assistance at Home, forc'd his Father to withdraw him from thence … Upon his leaving School, he seems to have given intirely into that way of Living which his Father propos'd to him …'till an Extravagance that he was guilty of, forc'd him both out of his Country and that way of Living which he had taken up.[6]

The historian, Alan Everitt has described the lifestyle of 'individual traders' in the late sixteenth century, who were willing to 'buy and bargain' any commodity that would make a profit:

> [They often] operated through a network of neighbours, friends and relatives. Sons, fathers, cousins … all were drawn into the circle … In consequence of this network of kinship and acquaintance …they had developed into a distinct and self-conscious community of their own: a kind of society of wayfarers … Much of the dealing in which travelling merchants engaged took place in … the provincial inn … Agreement between prospective dealers was rarely reached without a lengthy series

---

[4] See pages 140-142.
[5] See page 21.
[6] E.K.Chambers, *William Shakespeare: a Study of Facts and Problems*, Volume 2(1930), pp. 264, 265.

of 'speeches' and 'communications', and the company often sat far into the night before the transaction was concluded.[7]

In the Elizabethan period, before the development of professional theatres, inns were frequently used for staging plays.[8] Shakespeare and his father were probably intimately familiar with Elizabethan drama through John Shakespeare's wayfaring life style, particularly when visiting provincial and metropolitan inns.

Everitt concluded that the wayfaring community:

> Developed an ethos of its own dissimilar to that of the settled society of town and village. Its spirit of speculation and adventure ran counter to the stable traditions of the English peasantry ... it is not fanciful to trace a connection between the spread of private trading in the early seventeenth century and the rapid rise of Independency. For Independency was not a rural and static religion ... but mobile, virile, and impatient of human institutions, like the wayfaring community itself.[9]

Shakespeare scholars have always been puzzled by Shakespeare's acquisition of the language and sophistication necessary to write cosmopolitan plays of such quality. On the above evidence, he acquired such abilities through his participation in the culture of the wayfaring trading community associated with his father John Shakespeare.

Shakespeare's business activities should not therefore be seen only as a negative example of ruthless trading, but also providing a link to a highly cosmopolitan way of life. Many of his middle and upper class contemporaries were engaged in the same trading activity, and the late sixteenth century was a time of intense capitalist development.[10] This involved growing economic and social inequality, summarized by the historian Lawrence Stone as follows:

> As a result of population growth ... the excess supply of labour relative to demand not only increased unemployment, but forced down real wages to an alarming degree ... [there was] a polarization of society into rich and poor: the upper classes became relatively more numerous and their real

[7] See pages 22-24.
[8] F.E. Halliday, *A Shakespeare Companion 1564-1964* (1964), p. 243.
[9] See page 24.
[10] See L Neal and J.G. Williamson, *Capitalism: Volume 1: The Rise of Capitalism from Ancient Origins to 1848* (2014).

incomes rose; the poor became more numerous and their real incomes fell.[11]

In his personal life, Shakespeare had traversed a complete range of economic circumstances, from early comfortable family prosperity to dire poverty, and then wealth at the end of his life. It was this range of experience which gave him the understanding and breadth of knowledge which enabled him to write plays with such a universal appeal, although with some ambivalence when it came to attitudes towards the poor:

> But 'tis common proofe,/That Lowlynesse is young Ambitions Ladder,/Whereto the Climber upward turns his Face:/But when he once attaines the upmost Round/ He then unto the Ladder turns his Backe,/ Lookes in the Clouds, scorning the base degrees/ By which he did ascend.[12]

However, this ambivalence did not prevent him from expressing sympathy for the plight of the poor. The speech by two citizens in *Coriolanus* reveals considerable understanding of the anger of those suffering from famine when grain was being hoarded by the wealthy:

> … they nere car'd for us yet. Suffer us to famish, and their Store-houses cramm'd with Graine … If they would yeelde but the superfluitie while it were wholesome, wee might guess they releeved us humanely … our suffering is a gaine to them. Let us revenge this with our Pikes, ere we become Rakes.[13]

During the 1598 crisis, the poor of Stratford threatened violence against the rich, which no doubt Shakespeare was aware of.[14] The poor had appealed to the local magistrates for enforcement of the protective legislation, without realizing that all four magistrates were grain-hoarders, with strong links to the local townsmen. Shakespeare had become part of the local elite and no doubt felt threatened by the poor, who constituted nearly a half of the total population of Stratford.[15]

There has been a great deal of idealization of Shakespeare because of the outstanding quality of his writing. However, his sonnets indicate that he

---

[11] Peter Razzell, *Mortality, Marriage and Population Growth, 1550-1850* (2016), p. 107.
[12] See page 143.
[13] See page 144.
[14] See pages 141, 142.
[15] See page 142.

was tormented by feelings of inadequacy and a sense of alienation, but both the plays and sonnets demonstrate he was also a man of great sympathy and understanding. His business activities show that he was capable of ruthlessness, but this must be understood in the context of his times. He had restored the fortunes of his bankrupt family, at the same time creating the world's greatest literature. There is also evidence that he came to terms at the end of his life with the personal and social tensions reflected in his writings:

> Sweet are the uses of adversity, which like a toad, ugly and venomous, wears yet a precious jewel in his head. And this our life, excmpt from public haunt, finds tongues in trees, books in the running brooks, sermons in stones, and good in everything.

Peter Razzell

MR. WILLIAM

SHAKESPEARES

COMEDIES,
HISTORIES, &
TRAGEDIES.

Published according to the True Originall Copies.

LONDON

Printed by Isaac Iaggard, and Ed. Blount. 1623

William Shakespeare: The Anatomy Of An Enigma

by Peter Razzell

CALIBAN

This edition first published 1990
by Caliban Books
17 South Hill Park Gardens, Hampstead,
London, NW3 2TD

ISBN 1 85066 010 7

Typeset by Saxon Printing Ltd.,
Saxon House, Heritage Gate, Derby, DE1 1DD

Printed and bound in Great Britain by
Billing & Sons Limited, Hylton Road,
Worcester, WR2 5JU

To Josephine and Luke, my daughter and son
– and to the memory of my fellow sociologist,
Stephen Schenck

ACKNOWLEDGEMENT

I would like to acknowledge valuable contributions made by Miss Wretts-Smith and Miss Joyce Batty in translating Latin documents; and Christine Spence, Edward Razzell, Lorna Read and Jeremy Ward for their comments on the book and help with proof- reading.

Photographs were taken by Christine Spence and Canton Studios, Kentish Town. The Victoria and Albert Museum kindly allowed photographs to be taken of the Sheldon Tapestry Map and supplied the photograph used in Plate 11.

CONTENTS

CHAPTER 1: INTRODUCTION

In 1657, Thomas Plume, Archdeacon of Rochester, wrote about Shakespeare: "He was a glover's son – Sir John Mennis saw once his old Father in his shop – a merry Cheekd old man – that said – Will was a good Honest Fellow, but he durst have crackt a jeast with him at any time."[1] This description of Shakespeare's relationship with his father, is virtually the only direct personal account that has come down to us, and tantalisingly, illuminates a small fragment of Shakespeare's enigmatic biography. The major aim of this book is to unravel this enigma: to reveal the private face behind the public image, and to discover the person obscured by literary mythology. This can be viewed as "a quest for Shakespeare" – unravelling a series of strands which bring us nearer to an understanding of the man and the major events which shaped his life and writing.

The relationship which had the most influence on him, and had the greatest impact on his writing, was that with his father, John Shakespeare. The first half of the book will be about John Shakespeare – including his relationship with his son – and the central thesis of this part of the book can be stated as follows: the character of John Falstaff was based directly on Shakespeare's father, helping to explain not only key events in John Shakespeare's life, but also critical experiences in Shakespeare's own biography. Not only does this thesis help illuminate the Falstaff plays – *The Merry Wives Of Windsor*, *Henry IV, Parts 1 & 2* and *Henry V*, but also a number of the other works, including *Hamlet*. The second half of the book will focus on Shakespeare's own life independently of his father's – but even here, I will argue, John Shakespeare cast a long shadow over his son's life, including a history of alcoholism.

Although all the documentary evidence for a biography of Shakespeare and his father will be scrutinized in careful detail, and this will be supplemented wherever appropriate by evidence from the plays and poems, one additional major source of evidence will be used: that derived from sociological research. This has been carried out in the belief – along with C.Wright Mills – that the "sociological imagination" has a crucial role in explaining personal biography. Elements of economic and social history have been used by previous biographers of Shakespeare, but this has not been done in a systematic fashion. Much new work has been carried out in the last few years, using a more sociological approach to history, and this can illuminate biography, sometimes in quite a vivid way. For example, Shakespeare married Anne Hathaway when he was eighteen and she was twenty-six. Previous biographers have thought of her as an "older woman" – yet recent research has shown that the average age of first marriage of women in rural areas surrounding Stratford was about twenty-five, whereas the average age for men in Stratford was twenty-seven. From this we can conclude that it was not so much that Anne Hathaway was an "older woman", but rather that Shakespeare was a "younger man", compared to his contemporaries marrying during the same period.

This is a relatively minor example of the use of a sociological perspective, and a further example will help illustrate a more major theme. Shakespeare has always been thought of as coming from a narrow provincial background, which has been one of the difficulties in accepting his authorship of the plays. His father is known to have been a glover and probably a butcher at one stage of his career. The idea that the man who wrote some of the greatest plays ever written, should have been the son of a butcher – and even apprenticed to that butcher – just seemed too unbelievable to some Shakespeare admirers. I will be arguing later that this represents a misunderstanding of Shakespeare's Stratford experience; but more importantly, it was not realised until recently, that John Shakespeare was not merely a Stratford artisan, but in fact was a trader operating on a large scale, buying and speculating in a number of commodities (including the lending of money), and operating over a wide geographical area, including London.

This type of trading activity – designated by Everitt as "individual free trading" – gave rise to a particular way of life, with distinct and separate cultural values. In particular, these traders were highly cosmopolitan and lived not only in a provincial world, but operated in a metropolitan cultural setting. This helps to explain how Shakespeare came to acquire the cultural knowledge which enabled him to write plays of such universal appeal. But this conclusion can only be reached by examining a great deal of economic and social historical evidence, as will be the case with a number of the other themes in the book. At times, it will be necessary to switch from the realm of the personal and the biographical, to a more abstract sociological level, but in every case, the discussion of detailed economic and social historical evidence will lead to a greater understanding of Shakespeare's life and work.

Although a sociological perspective is central, much of the book is devoted to Shakespeare's more personal development. This has been undertaken through a careful examination of the known documentary material, linked to a textual analysis of a number of the plays. The linkage between biography and textual analysis is necessarily speculative and clearly must be approached with great caution, if only to avoid the imaginative but fanciful and untestable speculations that have marred much Shakespeare scholarship. Such a linkage can only be justified if it illuminates a major and central aspect of Shakespeare's life and work, while at the same time following the documentary and textual evidence in rigorous detail.

Far too many works on Shakespeare have been marred by excessive idealisation of their subject, illustrated by the recent tendency to use the Chandos portrait, rather than the well-attested Folio illustration or the bust of Shakespeare placed in Stratford Church by his wife and daughters. One critic complained that the latter made Shakespeare look like a "self-satisfied pork butcher"; the fact that his father was probably a butcher (among other occupations), and that Shakespeare was apprenticed to his father, seemed to have escaped this critic. For such scholars, the Shakespeare that they venerate, must appear as a figure matching his literary stature – perhaps understandable in an age when most of our traditional "gods" have been found wanting. And it is perhaps for this same reason, that the move to deny Shakespeare's authorship of the plays (in spite of overwhelming evidence to the contrary) has flourished. Although some of this is a form of class snobbery – how could a butcher's son and apprentice write such great works of art? – I will be arguing (as we have seen above), that Shakespeare's background was much more cosmopolitan that previously realised.

A good biography must include "warts and all", but excessive denigration is just as undesirable as excessive idealisation: any biography of Shakespeare must scrupulously follow the known documentary, legal and oral-historical evidence. Where the plays are used as a source of evidence – as they are in this book – it is important that material selected is used systematically, and not just in isolated fashion to buttress a particular case. It is for this reason that I have quoted extensively, and often *verbatim* from the plays and poems, allowing the material as much as possible, to speak for itself.

It could be argued that it is an error to assume that the plays can be used as a source of biographical material, when in fact they were written for a public and commercial audience. It could be further argued that the plays were a product of historical, cultural, political, literary, psychological and philosophical forces of such complexity, that they do not lend themselves to biographical analysis. It is self-evidently true that Shakespeare's plays are highly complex in their origin, with innumerable factors shaping their content and nature. But this should not deter us from focussing on particular aspects of the work; no analysis or criticism would be possible without specialist focus, and if at times this involves discussing material out of context, this can be justified if it adds to our understanding of the author and his work. Of course characters in the plays are not real people and they were put there by Shakespeare mainly for dramatic purposes, but I hope to show that particular plays were of special autobiographical significance, and that certain characters – in particular Falstaff – were of central importance in Shakespeare's own life. This does not mean that there can be any literal translation of character into biographical reality, but it does mean that certain characters can reveal important truths about a writer's life, and if taken in this spirit, can illuminate the author both as a man and a writer.

From Ben Jonson onwards, critics of Shakespeare's work have noted the imaginative, free-flowing quality of the plays, with frequent errors of historical fact and logical inconsistencies in plot and structure. Many of the plays have an almost dream-like quality, and can be seen (to use Freud's phrase) as "over-determined", with multiple determinants of content, including a biographical dimension. In some instances, this has been widely ackowledged; for example the "little eyases" passage in the Folio edition of *Hamlet*, which is universally recognized as a reference to the influence of the children's theatre. It is a good example of how Shakespeare used material of personal significance, and introduced it into the texture of the play, as if it were an intrinsic part of the drama. This only becomes obvious where the material is of a relatively public nature, and it becomes more difficult to recognize passages of private personal significance, particularly where the material is "unconscious", although we tread on notoriously dangerous ground with this potentially lethal concept. One of the characteristics of Shakespeare's work is that he will often take a theme – for example the issue of the morality of pre- marital conception in *Measure For Measure* – and work it, and re- work it, through various characters and sub-plots: and very often these thematic repetitions are of autobiographical significance.

Unfortunately, Freud, Ernest Jones and other psychoanalysts writing on Shakespeare, applied the psychoanalytical method purely speculatively, and in such a manner as to make any empirical evaluation difficult. Although the psychological analysis of a particular theme in a dramatic work is sometimes productive, it is necessary to assess the effect of other factors which might account for the phenomenon in question. For example, the character of Falstaff is largely an invention of Shakespeare's, and not a reflection in detail of a known historical or literary character, but this conclusion can only be reached through an examination of the historical and literary evidence. This cautionary process is well-understood, being so near to self-evident common-sense, but it is not so well-understood from the other side, i.e. the importance of checking purely literary and historical conclusions against psychological considerations. An important example perhaps of this is the question of the date on which *Hamlet* was written. There has been much scholarship and analysis of historical and literary source material, but as far as I know, no detailed discussion of an important psychological fact, the date of Shakespeare's father's death, and how this might fit into the known chronology of the writing of the play.

An appeal to examine all forms of empirical evidence in testing ideas will command universal assent, but some of the speculation in this book will predictably provoke a critical response. The justification for speculation exists where it is possible to test at least part of the ideas through further historical research. Much speculation takes place tacitly, with biographers decrying the validity of using the plays as a source of biographical material, and then proceeding to do just that, albeit in a piecemeal rather than a systematic fashion. Random historical and empirical research is unlikely to throw up much new material on Shakespeare's life, whereas the systematic search for material directed by particular hypotheses may well lead to important discoveries.

An example of this is the oral tradition of Shakespeare poaching deer from Sir Thomas Lucy; this tradition has been viewed with scepticism by some Shakespeare biographers, largely on the ground that there is no evidence that Sir Thomas Lucy owned a deer park at the time. But an examination of the plays makes it clear how important this incident was to Shakespeare (references to killing deer are to be found in eighteen of the plays). Because of this, a detailed search was made for further evidence, resulting in the discovery of much new important material. I will argue that being caught and punished for this, had a profound effect on his subsequent development, particularly in leading to his exile from Stratford and creating the reaction against his youthful wildness. Much of this new evidence is on deer parks owned by Sir Thomas Lucy, and although highly detailed and at times quite technical, I hope this will make a substantive contribution to Shakespeare biography.

This example of the poaching tradition also illustrates one major weakness in existing Shakespeare scholarship: many biographers have been primarily interested in the literary aspect of Shakespeare's life, and as a result have tended to take a "metropolitan" view, and therefore been somewhat disdainful of the oral tradition, which has invariably been locally based. (It is perhaps for this reason that there has been no definitive scholarly study of the history of Stratford- on-Avon – all the more remarkable when we remember the vast amount of material which has been collected on the town, lending itself eminently to new historical techniques and methods of research.) Malone was a major example of this, listing the various errors he believed that Rowe had made in his biography based mainly on oral sources. In fact, Rowe has stood the test of subsequent scholarship remarkably well, in particular with his knowledge of John Shakespeare's occupation as a wool dealer, his information on Shakespeare's wife's maiden name, and I will be arguing in this book, his description of the young Shakespeare's poaching activities. Many scholars have on general grounds decried the value of the oral tradition, and then have proceeded to smuggle it into their argument to buttress a particular thesis. Given the paucity of information on Shakepeare's life, a general principle for the use of the oral evidence – at least that which derived from living memory – should be that it is to be treated as valid, until proved otherwise.

That the oral tradition could span long periods is shown by Richard Gough's vivid recollections on the lives of the people of the village of Myddle, Shropshire, written at the end of the seventeenth century, and published in *The History Of Myddle*.[2] Gough in his accounts of individual families, occasionally spanned a period of nearly two hundred years, showing that at least for a village in Shropshire, the oral tradition was very strong indeed. And Gough's delightful language gives us historical insight into the cultural world that helped shape Shakespeare. Those who find it difficult to believe that Shakespeare could have written the plays, do not understand the richness of this oral tradition, which can be documented from at least Gough through to Henry Mayhew and beyond. In fact, I would argue, it is difficult to imagine the plays being written by anyone not educated in this tradition, and this is particularly true with respect to the great popular comic characters, such as Falstaff.

Bold hypotheses following known evidence are not in themselves sufficient: for an idea to be worthwhile it must be testable through future documentary research. It is the nature of this book, that it lends itself to detailed factual scrutiny, particularly with respect to the character and nature of John Shakespeare's associates in later life. For example, John Shakespeare's two friends and associates John Audley and Thomas Cooley, acting for surety for John Shakespeare and each other in the Queen's Bench Court in 1580 – further research on these two figures will shed considerable light on John Shakespeare's character and behaviour. Hopefully, there are a number of ideas in this book which will lend themselves to critical scrutiny, so that the book's conclusions will be open to future evaluation. Whether or not subsequent research validates all elements of this book, it is hoped it will make a stimulating and provocative contribution to Shakespeare scholarship. In the last resort, the interest of the book will derive from all our fascination with the man who produced some of the greatest written works of art in the English language. If it adds to our understanding of the man and his work, it will be worthwhile.

CHAPTER 2:
THE RISE OF JOHN SHAKESPEARE

Other than the sole brief contemporary description of John Shakespeare, the evidence for his biography is exclusively documentary. Halliday has summarized this evidence in his *Shakespeare Companion*, as follows:

> "**Shakespeare, John** (d.1601), son of Richard Shakespeare, and the poet's father must have left Snitterfield sometime before 1552, when he is first mentioned in the Stratford records, he, Humphrey Reynolds and Adrian Quiney each being fined 12d. for making a dunghill in Henley Street, where presumably he was living. In a suit of 1556 he is first called a 'glover', a trade he followed until at least 1586, when he again appears as a glover; he did not sign his name, but made his mark, sometimes in the form of a pair of glovers' dividers. He also traded in barley, timber and wool, and possibly other commodities. In other documents he is styled 'yeoman', that is, a man of substance under the degree of gentleman. The twenty years of 1556-1576 are years of prosperity:
>
> 1556. Buys two houses; the 'Woolshop' in Henley Street and another in Greenhill Street.
> 1557. Marries Mary Arden, daughter of his father's landlord at Snitterfield.
> 1558. Birth of his first child, Joan. (Six other children were born 1562-74, and Edmund in 1580.)
> 1557-62. Successively borough constable, affeeror (assessor of fines), and chamberlain.
> 1561. Administers his father's estate.
> 1564. Birth of William Shakespeare.
> 1565. Alderman; 1568 Bailiff (mayor); 1571 Chief Alderman and J.P.
> 1575. Buys two more houses; sites unknown, but probably the Birthplace, and an adjoining house to the west, destroyed in the fire of 1594.
>
> The twenty years of 1576-96 appear to be years of adversity.
> 1577. He ceases to attend council meetings.
> 1578-9. Mortgages his wife's Wilmcote property, lets Asbies, and sells her share in the Snitterfield estate.
> 1580. Fined £40 for failing to appear before the court of Queen's Bench to

give security that he would keep the peace.
1586. Replaced by another Alderman because 'Mr Shaxpere dothe not come to the halles when they be warned, nor hathe not done of long tyme'.
1587. Sued for part of the debt of his brother Henry.
1592. Included in a list of recusants 'for not cominge monthlie to the churche . . . It is sayd . . . for feare of processe for debtte'.
His fortunes are restored 1596-1601 probably by the poet:
1596. The Grant of Arms.
1597. His son William buys New Place. Attempts to recover the mortgaged estate from John Lambert.
1599. Applies for leave to impale the arms of Arden.
1601. Again appears as a member of the borough council. On 8 September, 'Mr Johannes Shakepeare' was buried in Stratford churchyard."[1]

Very little has been added to our knowledge of John Shakespeare since Halliday wrote the above, except for a recent and very important discovery about his economic activities, made by D.L.Thomas and N.E.Evans and published in 1984. This will be discussed in some detail later, but the scale of John Shakespeare's transactions – he made loans of £180 in 1568, and bought wool worth £210 in 1571 – sharpens the enigma which has fascinated all scholars familiar with Shakespeare's father's biography: the sudden transition in status from prosperous, successful, and respectable Stratford burgher to impoverished corporation and church absentee. As Thomas and Evans have written in the light of their findings about his prosperity in the early 1570's: "All the more surprising then, is his fall from public position later in the 1570's. Having attained the highest elective office that Stratford had to offer, John Shakespeare withdrew from borough life after 1576; he ceased attending meetings of the council and was ultimately removed from his position as alderman. At the same time, he got into debt and sold land. His decline was dramatic but is as yet unexplained."[2]

★ ★ ★

In order to analyse this dramatic decline we must first examine John Shakespeare's economic history in as great a detail as the documentary evidence will allow. It has already been noted that his main trade was that of glover, and it is this occupational description that is applied to him in most contemporary records. (He is also described as a "whittawer" – defined as someone who turns skins into white leather.) However, he was also a dealer in wool and a moneylender, as well as someone who bought and sold timber, barley, and according to Lee, sheep, skins, meat and leather.[3] The documentary record is confirmed by Shakespeare's earliest biographers, Aubrey and Rowe, who deriving information from local Stratford inhabitants, wrote that John Shakespeare had been a dealer in wool (Rowe) and a butcher (Aubrey).

In retrospect, Shakespeare's father's multiplicity of activities should not surprise us; Stratford had grown up as an agricultural marketing town, serving a wide area of midland towns and surrounding counties, stretching through Gloucestershire, Oxfordshire, Staffordshire, Cheshire, Lancashire, Shropshire and Wales.[4] Nearly all agricultural products were traded through the town – corn, seed, horses, cattle, and as we shall see later most importantly of all, barley and malt.[5] Other than the production of malt, the making of gloves and related products was probably the most important manufacturing activity in the Elizabethan and early Stuart period. The trade flourished during the late sixteenth century, culminating in the formation of the Glovers and Whittawers Company in 1606[6]; glovers occupied the most prominent position on market days, and some of the most eminent members of the corporation were glovers.[7] But focussing on John Shakespeare' trade as a glover, is quite misleading. As Lee has written about Stratford : "Small farmers lived there in number, and . . . they dealt in all the products yielded by the cultivation of land and stock. Thus, in 1597 George Perry, of Stratford, was described as engaging in, 'besides his glover's trade, buying and selling of wool and corn, and making of malt'."[8] And as Lee further points out, John Shakespeare cultivated far more land than the majority of his neighbours, having inherited land from his father in Snitterfield (the exact amount is not clear), as well as leasing fourteen acres of land called Ingon Meadow in 1570, and owning substantial land – about 86 acres – in nearby Wilmcote through his wife Mary's inheritance.

In order to understand John Shakespeare's economic situation, we must analyze it in the context of the very radical changes that were taking place in English society at the time. Population had begun to increase at the end of the fifteenth century, and by the middle of the sixteenth century was expanding very rapidly – probably largely due to the progressive elimination of the plague from the countryside. Wrigley and Schofield have estimated that population increased from 2,773,851 in 1541 to 4,011,563 in 1601: an increase of forty-five per cent.[9] According to their figures, the population grew most rapidly in the periods 1546-1556 and 1561- 1586, and this growth was associated with a rapid increase in the prices of agricultural produce. This can be illustrated by the changes in the price of wheat at Exeter, for which there is a series going back to the year 1316. Looking at the price by half-century, it was stable for the two hundred-year period 1316-1499, varying between 6.9 and 6.21 shillings a quarter; in 1500-49 it increased slightly to 8.28 – and then in the following half-century, 1550-99, it jumped dramatically to 22.72, and continued to increase in 1600-49 to 37.81, before stabilizing again in 1650-99 at 39.52.[10] Most of this increase was probably due to a growth of demand resulting from expanding population, although the influx of silver and the debasement of the coinage probably also played a part.

Overall, between the beginning and the end of the sixteenth century, the price of grain rose sixfold and cattle and sheep by five times – the latter being typical of an increase in the prices of a basket of twenty-five consumer goods during the same period.[11] Prices of most products rose steadily throughout the whole of the sixteenth century, although there were some variations in particular decades. Cattle and sheep prices increased steadily and progressively throughout the whole of the sixteenth century, and this was also largely true of the products that John Shakespeare was trading in: wool and sheepskins. The latter had jumped in price in the 1560's – more than doubling in a decade – but continued to rise steadily thereafter; the former moved more erratically, and can best be charted by the following indices (1450-99 = 100): 1540-49: 153; 1550-59: 206; 1560-69: 205; 1570-79: 234; 1580-89: 225; 1590- 99: 315.[12] Wool prices were not only affected by domestic demand, but also by exports, and although the latter probably fell during the 1560s, they increased by about ten per cent in the next decade, changes reflected in the price of wool. There is no indication in these figures that John Shakespeare's economic problems were due to falling prices and a lack of demand for wool; on the contrary, the decade when he ran into difficulties – the 1570's – wool prices rose by over fourteen per cent.

The increase in population and the general level of prices led both directly and indirectly to a sharp polarization in the distribution of wealth, with some groups becoming very much richer and others poorer – with an additional growth in the absolute numbers of the poor. That this polarization did not become more extreme was largely due to the innovation in farming methods. It is a matter of controversy as to whether these changes constituted an "agricultural revolution", but there is general agreement that grain yields did increase, largely through the application of convertible husbandry, involving a mix of arable and pastoral farming. As a result, yields are estimated as having increased by 30% between 1450 and 1650.[13]

The above changes all refer to national trends, and there were of course significant regional variations, particularly in agricultural developments. Although there has been no detailed study of the economic and social history of Stratford and the immediately surrounding area, we are fortunate in having Skipp's study of five parishes within the Forest of Arden, some fifteen miles north of Stratford. Population increased rapidly during the late sixteenth century, from about 2,250 in the 1570's to 3,400 in 1650: an increase of the order of 50%; the rate of natural increase was particularly strong during the last quarter of the century – 45%. The price of arable produce trebled between 1530-59 and 1590-1619 (a slightly greater increase than the national average), whereas cattle and oxen more than doubled during the same period.[14] Rents in this area "often lagged behind prices to quite an extraordinary extent", and the result was a marked increase in the wealth "of the farmer: as against the landless labourer or craftsman on the one hand, and the landlord on the other."[15] This increasing wealth of farmers was not primarily due to improved methods of cultivation, but was a direct consequence of the much higher prices for their produce, at a time when rents were lagging very greatly behind prices. This was not the case in all areas of England – in some places landlords extracted rents in pace with the rate of inflation – and it was perhaps the absence of such pressure that led to the new agricultural methods not being introduced into the Forest of Arden until the early seventeenth century.

The effect of all these changes was the "Great Rebuilding" and "Great Refurnishing" of this part of Warwickshire; this was reflected most visibly in the proliferation of timber-frame farm-houses. From the study of local inventories, it emerges that houses with four or more rooms increased from 14% in 1530- 69, 41% in 1570-99, to 76% in 1600-24.[16] This was associated with a general change in the pattern of consumption: "increased personal wealth led to a rise in the demand for consumer products of every kind."[17] The simple, crude stools, forms, trestles and table boards of the mid-Tudor period, progressively gave way to joined tables, benches, turned chairs and bedsteads. The value of household goods increased by about 300%, and this included personal clothing: the number of garments per person nearly doubled between 1530-69 and 1570- 1609, an increase from an average of 6.4 to 11.4.[18] The latter growth in demand was directly relevant to John Shakespeare's trade as a glover and whittawer. This shift in consumption affected all household goods: between 1530-69 and 1610-49, the number of napkins listed in the inventories rose from an average of one to ten, table cloths from an average of one to two, flaxen sheets from three to six.[19]

The result was that the number of craftsmen increased significantly from the earlier period. Whereas in Tudor times many craftsmen were only part-time workers – working both as farmers and craftsmen – by the Elizabethan period there were large numbers of full-time craftsmen listed in the leather, textile, wood, building and metal trades.[20] Many of them were specialists – for example, in the building trade, sawyers, turners and joiners – and there was an associated rise in the quality of consumer products during the period. The changes not only applied to farming and craftwork but also to the whole structure of the economy; whereas in the earlier period, 1530- 69, only one in eight inventories specify ready cash, by 1610- 49 this had risen to one in three, and by 1650-89 eight in ten died with cash about them. Likewise, before 1575 there were no farmers owned monies lent out for interest, but by 1625-49 one in every four had risk capital out on loan.[21]

These changes occurred relatively late in the countryside, and the major development in trade and capital transactions took place in the rapidly growing towns, particularly London. An index of this is the change in the size of London's population, which according to Finlay was as follows: 1500: 50,000; 1550: 70,000; 1580: 100,000; 1600: 200,000; 1650: 240,000.[22] Although these figures are only very approximate, they do show a very rapid increase in the second half of the sixteenth century, particularly in the last two decades. London's population increased by nearly fifty per cent between 1550 and 1580, an indication of the growth of trading activity during John Shakespeare's most active years.

For Stratford itself, although we have no general economic and social history of the town, we are fortunate in having Martin's monograph on its demographic history for the Tudor and Stuart period. Using ecclesiastical and hearth tax returns, Martin has estimated that Stratford's population increased from 1,503 in 1563 to 2,597 in 1673 – an increase of 61.56%.[23] Although not quite so substantial an increase as the surrounding rural parishes, it nevertheless did grow very significantly over the whole period. There are no population figures available for the period we are most interested in: the latter half of the sixteenth century. It is possible to make very approximate estimates from the number of marriages; these increased from 173 in the period 1558-1568 to 195 in 1591-1601. Assuming a constant marriage rate, population would have increased by about 12.71% from 1563 to 1596 – a rate of increase of 0.41% per annum, slightly less than the 0.56% per annum found by Martin.

Most of the growth in the late sixteenth century period must have been due to immigration: an analysis of the parish registers reveals that the number of baptisms between 1558 and 1601 was 2,682, whereas the number of burials was only slightly less at 2,667[24] – a natural increase of only fifteen people over the whole period. A major reason for this lack of natural growth was the large number of burials due to plague; there were two main plague years in this period: in 1564 (the year of Shakespeare's birth) 259 people died – representing about a sixth of the total population – while in 1597, there was only a slightly lesser mortality, with 181 people dying.[25] (The mortality in this year may have been partly due to dearth in the grain supply.) Stratford's experience illustrates what was true of many English towns: plague and other diseases periodically decimated their populations, giving rise to a severe check on natural growth. London was the most outstanding example of this: its enhanced mortality meant that in order for its population to grow, it had to absorb about half of the natural growth of the whole country.[26]

From this and other evidence, it appears that Stratford shared in the prosperity of the area, functioning as it did as a market town covering the complete range of agricultural and other produce. The town had become thoroughly capitalistic in its economic structure and ethos; virtually all the leading townsmen and neighbouring gentry were engaged in the hoarding of barley and malt, in spite of contemporary national legislation and local council rulings against forestalling and engrossing.[27] On more than one occasion this nearly led to rioting during periods of poor harvest, and this will be dealt with in greater detail later in the book. In order to exploit the huge growth in profitability of farming, it was not enough to merely provide consumer goods and services for the surrounding population; most of the leading townsmen functioned not only as producers, but were also engaged in speculative activity. This can be illustrated by the example of Thomas Rogers, Bailiff of the Borough, who in 1595 was a butcher by trade, but was also engaged in extensive buying and selling of corn, malt and cattle.[28] John Shakespeare's multiple trading activities were not in themselves abnormal in Elizabethan Stratford, but the scale and scope of his ventures did differ from those of the average Stratford tradesman. This is so important for understanding John Shakespeare's economic position – and the way this shaped the milieu which in turn influenced Shakespeare's cultural world – that the whole subject will be considered in some detail.

★ ★ ★

John Shakespeare's father, Richard, probably lived for most of his life in Snitterfield, a village about three miles north of Stratford, and is known to have been a copyholder on one manor from at least October 1535 until October 1560, and a tenant on Robert Arden's land from 1528-60. When he died in 1561, Richard Shakespeare's goods and belongings were valued at £39.17s. – approximately £5,600 at current prices.[29] (The current value of all economic transactions will be indicated in brackets in order to appreciate the sums of money involved – all prices will be inflated by a ratio of 140, a minimal figure which is discussed in footnote 29.) Richard Shakespeare was a relatively prosperous husbandman, but like all small tenant farmers at this time, operated on a very modest scale. Skipp has summarized the position of farmers in the Forest of Arden : "The average fully inventoried summer farm for the period 1530- 69 is estimated to have covered about 33 acres, of which roughly a third (10 acres) was arable and two-thirds (23 acres) grass. In other words, the mid-Tudor peasant was growing corn almost exclusively for subsistance purposes; for profit he concentrated on animal husbandry."[30]

There is some uncertainty as to how much land John Shakespeare inherited from his father; nothing is known about his direct inheritance but there are two surviving documents referring to sales of land by John Shakespeare in Snitterfield to Robert Webbe in October 1579 for £4 (£560) and in Easter 1580 for £40 (£5,600).[31] This could either be a reference to two separate parcels of land, or a mistake in the price of the same plot of land – although from the wording of the documents, it looks as if the smaller plot was inherited from Richard Shakespeare, and the larger through John Shakespeare's wife, Mary Arden. What is clear, is that when John Shakespeare married Mary Arden some time before 1558, he inherited eighty- six acres of land at Wilmcote, near Stratford, which had been left to Mary by her father Robert Arden, Richard Shakespeare's landlord.[32] Soon after 26 November 1556, when Robert Arden made his will, John Shakespeare had probably acquired through marriage over 100 acres of land – and this put him into the category of a prosperous yeoman farmer by contemporary standards. However, he had moved to Stratford by 1552, and at that time was working as a glover, presumably after a seven-year apprenticeship in the town. He was probably born in about 1530 and so at the beginning of the 1550's, was a young man in his early twenties.

There is evidence that John Shakespeare had already commenced his climb to prosperity before his marriage to Mary Arden, for he had begun making investments and speculating in commodities previous to that date. In June 1556, he was sued by Thomas Siche, a husbandman from Arscote in Worcestershire, for a debt of £7 (£980) – and the case was resolved by default in John Shakespeare's favour. This dispute had led to violence but John Shakespeare had pleaded a use of just force on Siche – perhaps an indication of his strong and forceful personality.[33] In October, 1556, he bought two houses, one in Grenhill Street, presumably an investment, and the other in Henley Street – probably the house (East House) he had lived in since 1552, and bought in preparation for his marriage. In 1575 he paid £40 (£5,600) for the Middle and West Houses in what is now known as the Birthplace, and so his purchase of two houses in 1556 constituted a considerable outlay of money. (Another way of seeing this, is to set it against the incomes of various groups at this time: as late as 1688, Gregory King stated that a shopkeeper and tradesman's income was only £45 a year, with labouring people and out servants earning as little as £15.)

The first evidence of speculative activity on John Shakespeare's part, comes from a suit he bought against Henry Field, of Stratford, in November 1556 for the non-delivery of eighteen quarters of barley. Barley was fetching about £1 a quarter, and so this consignment was worth the very considerable sum of £18 – or about £2,500 at present values.[34] Prices of barley had increased significantly during the 1550's – rising from an index figure of 197 in 1540-49 to 450 in 1550-59[35] – and it appears that John Shakespeare was speculating in this commodity to maximize profits in a rapidly rising market. The engrossing and forestalling of barley and malt was commonplace in Stratford, and from the very beginning of corporation records, there is reference to such activity. In October 1555, the council prohibited inhabitants of the town from buying or storing barley for non-residents (although the storage of malt was allowed), and this presumably was enacted to create a monopoly for residents.[36] This was an era when trade was controlled and regulated, illustrated by the town's attitude to non-resident speculators buying corn on the open market : "no farrener beynge a badger shall not in eny on market day from henesforth lode ouer & above iij horysys but yt they

Brynge the Justice letteres for the safcondyt & ley vp no corne in peyne of £v."[37] This restriction on trade was to have very important consequences, in creating a new body of individual traders operating outside market towns – and we will see that Shakespeare's father was one of the first to trade in such a fashion.

John Shakespeare continued to be very active in local trade, and became embroiled in a number of legal disputes. Unfortunately, the details of all these are not known, partly because the Court of Record for which most evidence is available, dealt only with local issues, and very often only gave superficial information, particularly during the period 1570-84 when records were incomplete. Nevertheless, John Shakespeare was involved in twenty-five suits over a forty-year period, in sixteen of which he was the complainant and nine the defendant.[38] Where information is available, the evidence is that most of these disputes were for relatively small sums; this was because the court was purely a local one, and was used by tradesmen for collecting debts and settling other relatively minor matters.

It is only recently that it has been realized that John Shakespeare did not confine his business activities to Stratford, but ranged very widely, both geographically and economically. In 1984, Thomas and Evans published a summary of the findings of legal cases conducted in the Court of the Exchequer, which completely changes our perception of John Shakespeare's business life.[39] Four prosecutions were brought against him, two in 1570 alleging illegal loans, and two in 1572 for illegally dealing in wool. In 1570, all forms of money-lending for interest were illegal, and in order to enforce the law, the government rewarded informers by granting them a half share of penalties imposed upon offenders. The first informer was Anthony Harrison of Evesham, Worcestershire, who claimed in the formal information submitted on the 21st October 1569, that John Shakespeare had lent John Mussum of "Wulton" (Walton) in Warwickshire the sum of £100 (£14,000). The money was loaned some time after 26 October 1568, and the transaction was alleged to have taken place at Westminster; the money was to be repaid on or before the 1st November 1569, together with £20 (£2,800) interest – representing an annual rate of interest of 20%. No record of any subsequent proceedings has survived, and it is possible that Harrison and John Shakespeare settled out of court.

The second accusation was laid later in the same year by James Langrake of Whittlebury, Northamptonshire. He claimed that John

"Shappere alias Shakespeare", glover of "Stratford upon Haven", had lent John Musshem of Walton, Warwickshire £80 (£11,200) some time after the 25th October 1568, the loan to be repaid on or before 30th November 1568, with £20 (£2,800) interest – an exceptionally high annual rate of interest of about *260%*. The transaction also took place at Westminster, but in this instance, it was pursued to a conclusion; the judges of the Exchequer issued a writ to the sheriff of Warwickshire to bring John Shakespeare to court, but in the event, on the 3rd February 1570, he came to London of his own volition. Although denying guilt, he compounded with the court and was fined forty shillings. John Mussum was probably a business partner of John Shakespeare's. (Walton was just outside Stratford, and both Mussum and John Shakespeare were sued for debt in 1573 and 1578 by Henry Higford of Solihull, who had previously worked in Stratford as town clerk.) That both transactions took place at Westminster, on two consecutive days, and that the second one was for a very short period at a very high rate of interest, suggests that the loans were a part of a series of highly speculative and profitable ventures, made at very short notice.

Two years after the prosecutions for usury, John Shakespeare again suffered from the attentions of Langrake. In February 1572, Langrake claimed that John Shakespeare and John Lockeley, both of "Stretford super Haven", had illegally bought from Walter Newsam and others 200 tods of wool, at fourteen shillings per tod – a total purchase price of £140 (£19,600). The offence was committed on or after 26th February 1571, and again took place at Westminster. Later in the same year, Langrake claimed that John Shakespeare on or after the 1st September 1571 had bought at Snitterfield from Edward and Richard "Graunte" and others, 100 tods of wool at fourteen shillings a tod – a total purchase price of £70 (£9,800). There is no further record of these prosecutions, and it is probable that John Shakespeare compounded with Langrake in an out-of-court settlement. The prosecutions were brought under a statute of 1552, which allowed only manufacturers or merchants of the Staple to buy wool, and the potential penalty was the forfeiture of double the value of wool bought.

Not a great deal is known about the parties involved in these various prosecutions; virtually nothing is known about Anthony Harrison, except that he came from Evesham in Worcestershire. John Lockeley was another of John Shakespeare's partners, and was also a glover in Stratford-on-Avon; Richard Grant was Edward Grant's father, and they were members of a Catholic gentry family which owned an estate at Northbrook, near Snitterfied in Warwickshire – and will appear again later in the book. James Langrake was accused in 1570 of raping one of his servants, and attempted to intimidate his accusers by threatening to bring an accusation against them in the Exchequer – the outcome of the case is not known. In 1574 he was imprisoned along with eleven other informers for compounding with offenders without the agreement of the court, and in the following February he was fined £40 (£5,600) and banned from bringing further informations for a year.

Although usury was an offence under the law, it was essentially anachronistic. It had been practised widely during the medieval period, and had been legalized for a time during Henry VIII's reign. The law under which John Shakespeare was prosecuted was modified in 1571, with those lending under ten per cent only having to forfeit the interest if prosecuted. However, although usury can be seen as an outdated economic crime, it was still attracted great moral opprobium, and was a relatively rare practice in 1570 – only a total of 181 prosecutions for usury took place that year in the Exchequer, and as we have seen from Skipp's study of the Forest of Arden, none of the farmers' inventories showed money out on loan before 1575. In this respect, John Shakespeare's money-lending activities were something of an innovation in this area of Warwickshire.

It is important to realize that these speculative projects were not confined to the years 1568-71; we have already seen how John Shakespeare was buying barley in 1556, and continued to be embroiled in various disputes about money during the whole of his working life. In 1599 he sued John Walford of Marlborough in Wiltshire for non-payment of £21 (£2,940), John Shakespeare alleging that he had sold Walford twenty-one tods of wool at Stratford on the 4th November 1568, and that the £21 owing in cash had never been paid.[40] In 1571 he sued Richard Quiney (father of Thomas Quiney who married Shakespeare's daughter Judith in 1616) for £50 (£7,000)[41], and the following year brought a summons in the Court of Common Pleas against John Luther, which is sufficiently revealing to be worth quoting fully:

> "London. John Luther, late of London, glover alias John Luther of Banbury, Oxon., glover, was summoned to answer John Shaxbere of Stretford on Avon in co. Warwick, yeoman, in a plea that he owed him £50 (£7,000) etc. And John Shaxbere, by Henry Burr his attorney, said that John Luther on 16 June 13 Eliz. at London by a certain writing obligatory

> had acknowledged himself bound to the same John Shaxbere in the aforesaid £50 to be paid on demand. The said John Shaxbere had been damaged to the value of £10 (£1,400). And he produced there in Court the writing. And John Luther, by Thomas Gardener his attorney, came and defended force and injury, etc."[42]

The case went in favour of John Shakespeare and he was awarded 33s.4d. (£233) costs, but the significance of this document is that although John Shakespeare was probably unable to write – he signed all documents with a cross or his mark, a pair of glovers' dividers – he was capable of conducting complex transactions in writing, and therefore was presumably able to read. But perhaps more importantly, this case against Luther reveals the cosmopolitan nature of John Shakespeare's business life – engaged in dealings with someone who moved between London and Banbury, the transaction not only taking place in London, but also being brought to trial there. John Shakespeare had dealings with people living in London, Worcestershire, Northamptonshire, Oxfordshire, and, we shall see later, in Coventry, Nottingham and Stoke in Staffordshire. Most of his larger transactions took place in London – confirming the earlier emphasis on the importance of London as a trading centre – and this evidence totally changes our perception of John Shakespeare's world. His son William's background has always been thought of as a narrow provincial one, and this has been one of the difficulties in accepting Shakespeare's authorship of the plays. But John Shakespeare's life was anything but provincial, and we will now consider his economic and cultural world in some detail.

CHAPTER 3: JOHN SHAKESPEARE'S CULTURAL WORLD

In 1588, John Shakespeare made a submission in connection with a dispute with his nephew, John Lambert, over the sale of land, and included in that submission a reference to twenty pounds he claimed was owing to him. Most revealingly, he stated that he had "totally lost and failed to acquire the whole gain, advantage and profit which he by buying and bargaining with the aforesaid twenty pounds have had and acquired, to the loss of thirty pounds."[1] This is the credo – "buying and bargaining" – of the middleman, a group whose activities Everitt has designated, "the free trading between individuals".[2] He has defined this as the "type of bargaining which was mostly nearly 'free', or emancipated from official control: to dealing between individual traders, farmers and manufacturers in private."[3]

But before we consider the evidence that Everitt has published on the organisation and culture of this group of individual traders, we must examine information directly relevant to John Shakespeare's occupation as wool dealer. Bowden, in his definitive study of the wool trade in Tudor and Stuart England, provides us with the necessary background to understand John Shakespeare's transition from glover to wool-dealer. Writing about middlemen in the wool trade, Bowden tells us:

> "The second group of middlemen – the glovers, fellmongers, leathersellers etc – came to deal in wool through their interest in sheep skins, which they bought as a normal part of their business. When purchased from the farmer these skins were covered by a growth of fell wool, and this had first to be removed before the pelts could be put through the various processes of manufacture. As the wool was no use to the leather industry it was then sold (sometimes sorted according to quality) to wool dealers and manufacturers. From selling superfluous wool to dealing in fleece wool was but a short step to take; and in the second half of the sixteenth century the trade

in fleece wool of a few of the members of this group appears to have been as large as that conducted by many of the Staplers."[4]

And if we had any doubt that this applied to the Warwickshire area, Bowden goes on to state that the "glovers of the central and east Midlands . . . were great wool dealers."[5] Remnants of wool were found in John Shakespeare's Henley Street house (now known as the Birthplace), and part of this house was traditionally referred to in Stratford as 'the woolshop'; Bowden tells us that after the wool was bought, it was most frequently "carried to the dealer's house or wharehouse".[6] Along with the documentary evidence on John Shakespeare's dealings in wool, this extra information amply confirms the accuracy of Rowe's statement that John Shakespeare was a wool-dealer.

It is likely that John Shakespeare used sheep from the farms that he owned and leased for both fleeces and wool, and given that there were several references to him working as a butcher (this will be discussed later), he probably butchered as well as skinned sheep. In addition to the sheep from his own land, he was in a very good position through his contacts with farmers in the surrounding countryside – both his father and brother were small farmers – to gain ready access to other supplies of sheep. According to Bowden, one of the most important types of "wool growers were the husbandmen or 'petty breeders'. These small farmers, often living to the margin of subsistence, needed money with which to get in their harvests, to pay their rents, or simply to meet normal, everyday expenses."[7] Skipp has described the husbandmen of the Forest of Arden, with their thirty-three acre farms, two thirds of which were put down to grass to raise animals for cash – a natural source of supply for John Shakespeare's wool-dealing business.

But wool-dealing also contained the seeds of money-lending: "When a seller gave credit for wool he received a higher price for it than he would have done had he accepted payment in ready money. The price of wool sold on credit thus contained an element of interest . . . [and in] the sixteenth century this interest charge was normally disguised as part of the principal, but after the [Usury] Act of 1571 . . . it was sometimes recorded as a separate item."[8] And so John Shakespeare's business as a wool-dealer may well have directly led him into explicit money-lending ventures, although the evidence considered suggests that, quite independently, he had become one of Everitt's "individual traders", willing to "buy and bargain" any commodity that would make a profit.

Everitt has shown that this type of trading grew rapidly in the sixteenth century, particularly after about 1570. He has made a study of it through the records of disputes between traders in the Courts of Chancery and Requests, which provide a detailed picture of John Shakespeare's economic and cultural world. The majority of transactions took place privately in inns and farmhouses (to escape the trade restrictions such as those imposed by on corn buyers by Stratford Corporation), and were on a sufficiently large scale, to require goods to be delivered at a later date, frequently in several instalments. All were conducted on a credit basis, for which legal bonds were drawn up by a lawyer or scrivener. Many of the traders worked with partners, although these partnerships were very frequently only ephemeral arrangements. According to Everitt, because of the absence of banks, traders necessarily had to rely on their credit in the local community, and this often "operated through a network of neighbours, friends, and relatives. Sons, fathers, brothers, cousins, wives, uncles, mothers, brothers-in-law: all were drawn into the circle."[9]

In John Shakespeare's case, it does seem that he turned to neighbours, friends and relatives for financial help during periods of difficulty. Although there is no direct evidence that Shakespeare worked with his father on his trading activity, John Shakespeare did associate his son William with his legal suit against the Lambert family in 1588. Fripp argues very convincingly that Shakespeare showed "extraordinary knowledge, and large accurate usage, in his writings from the beginning, of legal terminology and procedure" (*Shakespeare: Man And Artist*, Vol.1, page 138), and it is probable that he worked for his father in drafting legal bonds for trading transactions. (Possibly under the tutelage of Henry Rogers, John Shakespeare's business partner and town clerk of Stratford?) Everitt has described the culture which grew up amongst individual traders:

> "In consequence of this network of kinship and acquaintance, the packmen, carriers, woolmen, and factors who engaged in the private agricultural market were not simply unconnected individuals. By the end of Queen Elizabeth's reign they had developed into a distinct and self-conscious community on their own: a kind of society of wayfarers, partially separate from the settled society of the manor house, a village, and market town. It must not be supposed that this society was altogether new; its origins went back to the medieval wool merchant, and perhaps beyond. But it was at the end of Elizabeth's reign, so far as the agricultural market is concerned, that it became a recognizable *community*, with its own characteristic customs, traditions, and ideals. Much of the dealing in which travelling merchants engaged took place in farmhouses. Some took place in

barns, and some in warehouses and corn-chambers. Perhaps the most characteristic meeting-place of the wayfaring community, however, was the provincial inn. The Elizabethan inn has no exact counterpart in the modern world. It was the hotel, the bank, the warehouse, the exchange, the scrivener's office, and the market place of many a trader."[10]

John Shakespeare's carried on many of his business meetings in London, and perhaps Everitt under-estimates the importance of London as the centre of internal trading. But with that caveat, and allowing for the relatively early period of John Shakespeare's trading, much of the above would apply to his case. No doubt many of his business meetings took place in the inns of Stratford and the surrounding area, although he was almost certainly familiar with the inns of Westminster and other areas outside the Stratford region. Everitt has elaborated on the role of the innkeeper in trading activities:

"The Tudor and Stuart innkeeper was thus in a powerful position to influence the course of private trading. Many a publican provided cellars or outbuildings for the storage of his clients' goods. Some converted their halls or parlours into private auction rooms. A few engaged in private dealings on their own account . . . Most innkeepers, however, confined their activities to 'finding chapmen' for customers and arranging bargains between two of his customers himself, as they were sitting at supper in the hall of the inn. Agreement between prospective dealers was rarely reached without a lengthy series of 'speeches' and 'communications', and the company often sat far into the night before the transaction was concluded. Sometimes an unscupulous innkeeper would allow some hapless yeoman (well plied with ale) to be 'cozened of his money' by the 'glozing terms . . . smooth words, and fair speeches' of the other party concerned; though no doubt most landlords, for the sake of their own reputation, endeavoured to encourage fair dealing. When the bargain was agreed, the local scrivener (sometimes himself one of the guests) was called upon to draw up one of the bonds, and the deed was read out to the assembled company."[11]

If this passage conveys the impression that the culture of the traders was defined solely by the inn and its practices, Everitt corrects this impression by bringing out the more spiritual side of their life:

"It is not surprising if the wayfaring community developed an ethos of its own dissimilar to that of the settled society of town and village. Its spirit of speculation and adventure ran counter to the stable traditions of the English peasantry . . . it is not fanciful to trace a connection between the spread of private trading in the early seventeenth century and the rapid rise of Independency. For Independency was not a rural and static religion, like anglicanism, nor rigid and urban, like presbyterianism, but mobile, virile, and impatient of human institutions, like the wayfaring community itself."[12]

Perhaps Everitt presents too ideal a picture of the independent trader's ethos and culture, but it does have the merit of pointing up the cosmopolitan and dynamic nature of this way of life. It also makes it much more comprehensible as to how Shakespeare acquired the cultural knowledge and background to write plays of such universal and general appeal. We will return to Everitt's work later in the book, as it provides one of the keys for explaining John Shakespeare's fall. Before leaving it however, we should note that Everitt does recognize that the activities of a trader like John Shakespeare were not always confined to one category; writing of "the conflicting aspirations of the market town and private trader", he notes that "many traders engaged in both spheres of activity, and it would be misleading to draw too sharp a distinction between them."[13] And this was particularly the case with Stratford: we will see later how most of the leading townsmen engaged in speculative trading in corn, and perhaps a majority of them could be categorized as individual traders during this period.

This can be illustrated by John Shakespeare's friend and associate, Adrian Quiney; he was a mercer by trade and lived in Henley Street (he was fined along with John Shakespeare for making an unauthorized dunghill in 1552). He and John Shakespeare served on the council together – they both held high office during the period of the reform of the Gild Chapel – and in 1571, when Quiney was bailiff and John Shakespeare was chief alderman, they "rode to London together on borough business, with permission from the aldermen and burgesses to proceed 'according to their discretions'."[14] Adrian Quiney was a business partner with his son Richard, and the correspondence between the Quineys and Abraham Sturley, reveals how widespread individual trading was in Stratford, with frequent references to loans, investments and possible speculative bargains.

An example of this is the loan/ business transaction that Richard Quiney sought to bring off with Shakespeare in 1598. Quiney appears to have been short of money, and in the first instance, sought a loan of £30 from Shakespeare. But a letter from Adrian to Richard in 1598 suggests a much broader possible arrangement, and is very revealing of local attitudes to money and trade : "Yff yow bargen with Wm Sha .. or receve money therfor, brynge youre money homme that yow maye; and see howe knite stockynges be sold; ther ys gret byinge of them at Aysshome. Edward Wheat and Harrye, youre brother man, were both at Evyshome thys daye senet, and, as I harde, bestow £20 [£2,800] ther in knyt hosse; wherefore I thynke yow maye doo good, yff yow can have money."[15]

We see here a direct link between the trading activities of John Shakespeare and his son William, and it is clear that such activities were the norm in Stratford, rather than the exception. The Quiney family was one of the most respectable in the town: they bore arms, had been long settled in the community, and were influential members of the corporation.[16] They were well-educated – Richard conducted much of his correspondence with Abraham Sturley, who had been educated at Queen's College, Cambridge, in Latin – and appear from the language of this correspondence, to have been strongly puritan. Nevertheless, along with all other leading townsmen, they frequently engaged in speculative activity (particularly in corn and malt), and Adrian's letter to his son Richard, brings out just how far they were involved in a bargaining mentality – although in the example quoted, they were buying and selling stockings for their mercer's business.

John Shakespeare in the earlier period was just as respectable and eminent in the town as any of the other residents. Starting in 1556, he was appointed to Stratford Corporation, and held office continuously until the 1570's: he was successively aletaster (1556), burgess (1557), constable (1558), afeeror (1559 and 1561), chamberlain (1561 and 1562), alderman (1565), high bailiff (1568-69), and chief alderman (1571).[17] It is true that he was fined for non-attendance in 1557 and probably at other times as well, but his overall record of attendance was as good as any other member of the council. He is known to have missed only one meeting of the corporation in the thirteen years that records were kept from 1564 to 1577.[18] By any standards, Shakespeare's father was a highly conscientious and active member of the town council, until his sudden withdrawal at the end of 1576 or the beginning of 1577. After that date, he ceased to attend, even though he was still nominally an alderman for another ten years.[19] John Shakespeare's role as a member of the corporation should not be exaggerated however: the council only met about once a month, and there are only thirty-two specific occasions when he is mentioned as attending in the eleven-year period 1566-77 (although there is only one occasion when he is listed as being absent.) There is no inconsistency between regular participation in corporation affairs, and life as an individual trader, including visits to London and elsewhere. In fact, he was prosecuted for usury and wool-dealing at the very time he had achieved highest office in Stratford – 1568-71 – when he was bailiff and chief alderman, and had visited London with Adrian Quiney on council business.

His last known date of certain attendance was on the 5th September 1576, thus suggesting he withdrew from corporation meetings sometime between the 5th September, 1576 and 23rd January, 1577. That this withdrawal was not made directly on economic grounds is indicated by a number of items of evidence. The following is recorded in the Minutes and Accounts of Stratford Corporation : "5th December 1576 – It is also ordered and agreed upon that every alderman shall pay (savinge Mr Lewes and Mr Plumley) xii.d. [£7] a pece this present yere towardes the wages of the common bedyll, and the said Mr Lewes and Mr Plumley to pay viii.d. [£4.65] a pece, and all the burgesses shall pay iiii.d. a pece this present yere savinge that Mr Nicholas Barnehurst shall pay for his part xii.d. towardes the wages of the said bedyll."[20] It was customary for the levies on burgesses and aldermen to be a reflection of their economic status; burgesses being in the main poorer than aldermen paid a third of the latter's levy, and individual aldermen, such as Mr Lewes and Mr Plumley paid less on account of poverty, or more in the case of Burgess Barnehurst because of his wealth.

At this critical time of Alderman Shakespeare's life, he was considered by his colleagues to be capable of paying the full levy for an alderman. But a year later, the position had changed dramatically: "29th January 1578: At this hall yt ys agreed that every alderman, except suche under wrytten excepted, shall paye towardes the furniture of three pikemen, two billmen and one archer vi.s. viii.d.[£47] . . . Mr Shaxpeare iii.s. iv.d.[£23.50] ..."[21] Up until this point, John Shakespeare had always been assessed in the normal way, and during the twenty years he had been associated with the council, he had if anything, loaned money to the corporation in his day-to-day business on their behalf. And here he was being levied at half the normal rate for an alderman – the first indication of his ensuing economic difficulties. He failed to pay this reduced levy, and was altogether excused on the 19th November 1578 from a weekly contribution of 4d. towards the relief of the poor.[22] During this same year, as we will see later, he began to sell and mortgage land which he had acquired through inheritance.

That his withdrawal from council meetings was not initially due to economic factors is further confirmed by current corporation practice; when a member of the council got into economic difficulty, the corporation either made reduced levies or allowed the member in question to resign on grounds of poverty, and this certainly happened to other members of the council.[23] In spite of John Shakespeare only attending once – as far as is known – during the ten years after 1577, no attempt was made to expel him from the council; but finally, on the 6th September 1586, it was noted in the corporation minutes, that "Mr Shaxspere dothe not come to the halles when ... warned nor hathe done of long tyme" – and he was expelled.[24] It is clear from this that it was not any antagonism on the part of the council – either on economic, religious or social grounds – that was responsible for his withdrawal; on the contrary, the corporation had been extraordinarily patient before expelling such a prolonged absentee, which presumably was a measure of their esteem given his previous twenty years of conscientious and valuable service.

The puzzle of the dramatic transformation in John Shakespeare's life is deepened when we examine his more general economic circumstances during this period. All the evidence is that he continued to enjoy prosperity and social position right up until the time of his withdrawal from the council; in October 1575 he bought two houses costing £40 (£5,600)[25], and more importantly, in about 1576 he applied for a grant of arms, which appears in part to have been successful. According to the commentary attached to the grant of arms made to Shakespeare senior in 1596, "This John shoeth a patierne under Clarent Cookes hand – paper xx years past."[26] As Fripp has pointed out, in order to apply for a grant of arms the applicant had to convince the relevant authority that he could live without "manual labour" and "bear the port, countenance and charge of a man of substance"[27], and apparently John Shakespeare successfully convinced the Clarencieux King-at-Arms Robert Cook that he was capable of this, as Cook did suggest an actual 'patierne' for a grant of arms. Clearly, John Shakespeare considered himself a sufficient economic and social success in about 1576 to warrant the title and social status of 'gentleman'.

One possible explanation for the sudden decline in Shakespeare senior's economic and social fortunes is ill-health – this in principle could account for both his sudden poverty, and his abrupt withdrawal from corporation meetings. However, when a councillor was sick he was excused attendance, with the explicit statement that the person was 'infirmus'[28] – and there was no indication in the language with which John Shakespeare was expelled – "dothe not come to halles when . . . warned" – that there was any presence of illness. However, there is one form of explanation that has attracted a great deal of scholarly interest, and which will be considered in some detail in the next section – that John Shakespeare was a religious recusant and withdrew from the council on grounds of religious persecution.

★ ★ ★

There have been two diametrically opposed religious explanations as to why John Shakespeare withdrew from corporation meetings: one that he was a Puritan, the other that he was Catholic. The most scholarly advocate puritan thesis is Edgar Fripp. Most of Fripp's evidence is taken from Stratford corporation records; in 1563 and 1564/1565 Shakespeare's father was active chamberlain for the borough, and made the following payments which were incorporated in his annual account: "10 Jan. 1564 – Item payd for defaysing ymages in ye chappell – 2s.; March 1565 – Item payd for taknge doune ye rood loft in ye chappell – 2s.; Item payd to Peter Start for workynge ye seattes – 6s."[29] These were typical puritan measures and there were other similar items of general expenditure on the chapel during this period, suggesting that the building was undergoing a structural reformation along Protestant lines. The chapel had originally belonged to the Gild of the Holy Cross, but became the property and official chapel of the Stratford Corporation in 1553 when the borough received its charter. (The corporation met in the Gild Hall adjoining the chapel, which was near the centre of the town, unlike the parish church which was on its periphery.) In 1571 when Shakespeare senior was Chief Alderman (deputy mayor) it was decided by the council that "Mr Adrian Queny (the mayor) ... shuld sell the copes and vesmentes", and later in 1573 when John Shakespeare was an ordinary alderman, the corporation arranged "for glasinge the chapell wyndowes".

It was on the basis of this and other evidence that Fripp concluded that John Shakespeare was a Puritan, and for this period when he was active on the council, the evidence certainly points in this direction. The conclusion has been disputed by other historians, such as Mutschmann and Wentersdorf, who have argued as follows: "At the end of 1563, the Guild Chapel . . . was Protestantized, and the images were defaced. John Shakespeare it is true, was a member of the corporation, and as Chamberlain had to pay the bills for the defacing; there is nothing, however, to indicate his personal views about this procedure, which was carried out in compliance with government instructions, and very tardily at that."[30] There are a number of problems with this argument: firstly, it ignores the fact that John Shakespeare was actively associated with nearly *all* the extensive changes in the chapel. Secondly, it is largely self-contradictory: the "lateness" of the reforms (and they were certainly later than elsewhere – London made orders for the destruction and sale of Catholic objects in 1559, Leicester in 1561[31]), would highlight the role of *John Shakespeare* in making the changes, i.e. suggesting that he took a major part of the initiative in carrying out reforms when he achieved office.

But the religious affiliation and attitudes of Shakespeare's father, can only be properly understood in the context of the religious and social life of the town, and as this is somewhat complex, I will attempt to summarize its relevant features. The corporation was the successor to the medieval gild, and acquired most of its property and much of its structure of authority from the gild. Additionally, its social life was partly determined by the nature of the gild; not only was the corporation considered a "brotherhood" – loyalty to the council by its members was a primary requisite – but it was also seen as a religious fraternity. Quoting Fripp: "On Leet Days, Fair Days, and certain other occasions, Aldermen and Burgesses attended in their gowns at his [the Mayor's] house to escort him to Church or through the market or in perambulation of the Borough boundaries. They wore their gowns at Church on Sundays and holidays, and had seats near the pulpit."[32]

There is no direct evidence about John Shakespeare's attendance at church during the period he was a member of the council, but we do know that he was one of the most active members of the corporation (certainly in terms of attendance at its meetings), and as Bailiff and Chief Alderman at different times, he would have attended church as a part of his official duties. But what is the evidence that Stratford was a puritan corporation, other than the information already quoted from council records? *The Victoria County History of Warwickshire* has summarized one reading of the evidence as follows: "The defacing of the images in the Gild Chapel, carried out when Shakespeare's father was chamberlain in 1563; the prohibition of stage plays in 1602, and the tone of the correspondence and wills of many of the leading townsmen all indicate the puritan atmosphere of Elizabethan Stratford."[33]

There is support for this conclusion from other sources; in January, 1575, Warwick Corporation wrote of the members of the Stratford Council that "they are men known of good credit, honest behaviour, upright dealing and such as upon their credits might be trusted"[34] – and coming from a body known for its strong puritan leanings, this must be taken as confirmation of the overall puritan nature of the Stratford Corporation. (Although in the light of the previous discussion of the importance of personal credit amongst traders, it is interesting to note the emphasis on credit-worthiness in this recommendation.) Likewise, when a survey of the ministry was made in Warwickshire in November, 1586, it was noted that the minister at Stratford, the Reverend Barton, was "a precher, learned, zealous and godlike and fit for the ministerie".[35]

But this image of a strongly puritan Stratford is misleading in some respects. The council throughout John Shakespeare's lifetime supported and paid for the performance of plays in the town virtually every year (in some years three or four companies of players were paid for[36]); the town entertained the players with drink and food at the local inns, The Bear and

The Swan, as well as entertaining local justices, visiting preachers and its own officers, and expenditure on wine was one of the chief expenses. However, during the Elizabethan period, the antagonism of puritans towards the theatre and drinking was not as strong as it was to be in the following century, and it has even been argued that during the early period of the Reformation there was a natural alliance between puritanism, the theatre and the drink trade – all antagonistic to the old Catholic authoritarianism and suppression of free discussion of new ideas and practices.[37] (Fripp has also pointed out that a number of the innkeepers in Warwickshire were of the puritan persuasion – not surprising given that many of them were acting as brokers and bankers for individual traders, many of whom were ardent Protestants.) And the behaviour of the leading townsmen in other contexts – legal disputes over debts, physical assaults and scurrilous personal attacks[38] – hardly suggests the sober and restrained respectability that we latterly associate with puritanism.

None of this however contradicts Fripp's argument that during the period that John Shakespeare was a member of the corporation he was at the very least sympathetic to the Protestant cause, and even possibly strongly in favour. Fripp uses this conclusion to go on to argue a much more contentious thesis as to why Shakespeare senior abruptly withdrew from the council, and suddenly appeared to lose economic status. Fripp's argument runs as follows: as a result of Bishop Whitgift's investigation of recusancy in Warwickshire in 1577, John Shakespeare became frightened and "went to earth" (withdrew from public life), and in order to cover up his recusancy he became "suddenly anxious to appear 'of no account', 'a very beggar', ready to plead 'debt' and 'fear of process', unwilling to pay his levies and fines . . . "[39] Fripp concluded that Shakespeare's father in effect went into hiding; he withdrew from public life and presented himself as a virtual bankrupt in order to escape the effects of prosecution for being a puritan recusant.

The evidence however when scrutinised in detail does not support Fripp's thesis: Bishop Whitgift did not institute his inquiry until *October 1577*[40], whereas John Shakespeare stopped attending corporation meetings some time between the 5th September 1576 and 23rd January, 1577, i.e. *about a year before Whitgift's enquiry*. It is true that the Grand Ecclesiastical Commission had been set up in April 1576 to amongst other things "order, correct, reform and punish any persons willfully and obstinately absenting themselves from church and service"[41], but as Fripp himself points out, the Commissioners were mainly concerned with "papists", and only acted were not started until October 1577. There is other even more important evidence against Fripp's thesis, but this will be considered at a later and more appropriate stage.

The alternative hypothesis, that John Shakespeare's withdrawal from the council and fall into poverty was due to his espousal of Roman Catholicism, has most forcibly been argued by Mutschmann and Wentersdorf: "The explanation of John Shakespeare's abrupt break with borough life must be sought . . . with the beginnings of the Catholic counter-reformation in England, the mission whose aim was to rouse Catholics from their easygoing attitude of outward conformity with the Anglican Church . . . Among those who responded by becoming open recusants voluntarily withdrawing from public life rather than take the forbidden oath of supremacy or attend Anglican services, was Alderman John Shakespeare."[42] Like Fripp, Mutschmann and Wentersdorf explain Shakespeare senior's economic difficulties as being the result of his religious recusancy; directly through the imposition of heavy fines, and indirectly through the attempt to avoid fines by handing over his property "for safekeeping to trustworthy friends", devising his "lands to tenants, friends or . . . relatives", some of whom turned out to be untrustworthy and refused to return this property after the pressure of religious persecution had lifted.[43]

Most of this argument is speculative, lacking any direct evidence or documentary confirmation. The only evidence solidly in its favour is the Catholic religious will and testament made in John Shakespeare's name, found in the loft of the Shakespeare Henley Street house in 1757. Although this document was in standard form, most scholars now accept that it is genuine, and that in all probablity John Shakespeare did die a Catholic.[44] But all the evidence is that this was a late conversion, for during the period that John Shakespeare was a member of the corporation, he actively supported the Protestant reformation of the gild chapel, and nowhere is there any mention of fines, difficulties, or religious persecution on Catholic grounds. The only mention of his "recusancy" is the inclusion of his name in the list of recusants for the year of 1592; but his name was very clearly grouped with eight others who were stated as "not comminge monthlie to the churche . . . It is sayd . . . for feare of process for debtte", and there is good evidence that all nine people on this list were in deep economic difficulty at this time[45], and none of them appear on the recusancy roll for 1593.[46]

Others in the 1592 recusancy survey were explicitly listed as avoiding church because of their Catholic affiliations, but John Shakespeare was not one of them. He had good reason to fear arrest for debt: in 1589 William Burbage had sued him in the London Court of Common Pleas for the recovery of £7 (£980) awarded him in 1582, and was granted his suit, with 35 shillings damages (£245).[47] The original suit had arisen out of the leasing of a house by John Shakespeare, the £7 apparently being the sum that Burbage had originally paid for the lease (one must assume that John Shakespeare did not fulfill his part of the bargain). The older Shakespeare did not pay this debt or the damages arising out of the 1589 case, and an initial warrant for his arrest was issued after he failed to appear before the Justices of the Common Pleas in April, 1592.[48] As Eccles has concluded: "Shakespeare's father had good reason to fear arrest, for he had never paid the debt of seven pounds and damages which William Burbage had never recovered from him in 1589."[49]

Both Fripp and Mutschmann & Wentersdorf make a great deal of the transfer of land by John Shakespeare to friends and relatives, allegedly to avoid the effects of religious persecution. Both groups of authors argue that Shakespeare's father was cheated out of land in this way, and they particularly had in mind the mortgaging of the land inherited through Mary Arden at Wilmcote in the parish of Aston Cantlow. Shakespeare senior mortagaged this land to his brother-in-law Edmund Lambert (he was married to Mary Arden's sister) in 1578, and this transaction and its aftermath is of such central importance for understanding John Shakespeare's character, that the next chapter will be devoted entirely to a discussion of it.

CHAPTER 4: THE SHAKESPEARE/LAMBERT DISPUTE

The first surviving legal document relating to the Shakespeare/Lambert land transactions is the foot of fine registered in Easter of 1579. The relevant substance of this document is as follows

> "This is the final agreement made in the court in Westminster ... Between Edmund Lambert complainant and John Shakespeare and his wife Mary defendants concerning two messuages two gardens fifty acres of land two acres of pasture four acres of pasture and common of pasture of all sorts of beasts with appurtenances in Aston Cantlow whence a plea of agreement had been summoned between them in the same Court. That is to say that the aforesaid John and Mary recognized the aforesaid tenement and common pasture with the appurtenances to be the right of . . . Edmund and his heirs in perpetuity . . . and for this recognizance concession quitclaim warrant fine and concord the same Edmund gave the aforesaid John and Mary forty pounds sterling."[1]

On the face of it, this was a straight sale of about 56 acres of land by the Shakespeares to Edmund Lambert for £40 (£5,600). The references to complainant and defendant were standard sixteenth century legal terminology; as Lewis has put it, "one of the legal methods of conveying and alienating land in the sixteenth century . . . was a fictitious suit in which one party sued the other for wrongfully witholding a given property. The defendant admitted the fictitious fact, and then the complainant paid the defendant for giving the premises back to him."[2] No mention was made in this foot of fine to any mortgage arrangement, and there was no reference to the land in question being held by other parties under lease; in fact the land was both mortgaged and let under lease.

In November 1579 a foot of fine was registered on a lease on land in Wilmcote owned by the Shakespeares. There has been much confusion and disagreement among Shakespeare scholars as to the significance of this lease, and its salient features run as follows:

> "Between Thomas Webbe and Humphrey Hooper, the complainants, and John Shakespeare and Mary his wife and George Gibbs, the defendants, concerning seventy acres of land, six acres of meadow, ten acres of pasture and common of pasture for all manner of animals with the appurtenances, in Wilmcote . . . That is to say: the aforesaid John and Mary and George recognized the aforesaid tenements and common of pasture, with the appurtenances, to be the property of . . . the same Thomas and Humphrey [held] as a gift of the aforesaid John and Mary and George . . . And for this recognition . . . the same Thomas and Humphrey granted to the aforesaid George the aforesaid tenements and common of pasture . . . from the feast of Saint Michael the Archangel [29th September] . . . one thousand five hundred and eighty, even to the end of a term of twenty-one years ...; he to render therefrom annually to the aforesaid Thomas and Humphrey, and to the heirs of Thomas himself, one-half of a quarter of wheat and one half of a quarter of barley to be paid annually on the feast-day of the Nativity of our Lord . . . The above-mentioned Thomas and Humphrey furthermore (had) granted to the above mentioned John and Mary a reversion of the above mentioned tenements and common of pasture, with the appurtenances, and the above-mentioned revenue previously reserved, and they (had) restored these to them in the same Court, to have and to hold by the same John and Mary, and the heirs of Mary herself . . . in perpetuity."[3]

This lease can only properly understood when its purpose from the Shakespeares' point of view is made clear; this will be discussed later, but for the moment we can note: 1. That Thomas Webbe and Humphrey Hooper in effect leased the land from the Shakespeares until the 29th September, 1580 – and this was achieved through fictional devices of complainant/defendant and gift/counter-gift. 2. That after this date in 1580 the land was leased for twenty-one years at a peppercorn rent to George Gibbs, who was almost certainly acting as the Shakeapeares' agent and steward.[4] In 1588 John Shakespeare lodged a bill of complaint against Edmund Lambert and revealed a mortgage which had been arranged in 1578. It is such a significant document for the reading of John Shakespeare's character, that it will be quoted very fully:

> "John Shakespeare complains . . . that . . . Edmund (Lambert) during his lifetime, to wit, on the fourteenth day of November (1578) . . . through a certain indenture bearing the date and the year aforesaid, had bought for himself and his heirs from the aforementioned John Shakespeare and Mary his wife one messuage or tenement, one virgate of land, and four acres of arable land with the appurtenances in Wilmcote in the said county of Warwick, to have and to hold . . . forever; provided always that if the said John Shakespeare, his heirs, executors, administrators or assigns either

> paid or caused to be paid to the aforesaid Edmund forty pounds of legal English money on the day of the feast of Saint Michael the Archangel [29th September] . . . one thousand five hundred and eighty, that the then aforesaid indenture and all things therein would be void; by virtue of which the same Edmund entered the aforementioned tenement with its appurtenancies, and from that time had possession of it as master from a fief, and thus remaining in possession from that time on, afterwards, to wit, on the first day of March (1587) . . . he died . . . after whose death the aforesaid messuage and other premises with the appurtenances descended to the aforesaid John Lambert, as son and heir of the said Edmund; and the said John Lambert, doubting his estate and interest of and in the aforesaid tenements with appurtenances to be void, and having knowledge that it was the purpose and intent of the said John Shakespeare to summon him to justice on account of the property, in consideration that the aforesaid John Shakespeare did not at once summon to court the said John Lambert on the account of the aforesaid tenment and the rest of the premises with the appurtenances, and (in consideration) that the said John Shakespeare and his wife Mary together with William Shakespeare their son, when claim had been made upon them, covenanted the said tenements and the other premises with appurtenances to said John Lambert and delivered all writings and proofs concerning the aforesaid premises; the aforesaid John Lambert . . . in consideration thereof took obligation upon himself and then and there faithfully promised that he, the same John Lambert would fully and faithfully pay and make satisfaction (to the amount of) twenty legal pounds in English money [£2,800]... the aforesaid John Lambert, however, caring but for the least for his aforesaid promise and undertaking, but with scheming and fraudulent intent craftily and cunningly to deceive and defraud this John Shakespeare of the aforesaid twenty pounds, has not up to this time paid the same twenty pounds . . . on account of which, the same John Shakespeare totally lost and failed to acquire the whole gain, advantage and profit which he by buying and bargaining with the aforesaid twenty pounds have had and acquired, to the loss of thirty pounds to John Shakespeare. And thereafter he brings a suit of law . . . and the same John Lambert defends the force and injury since etc, and says that he did not assume for himself in the way and form in which the aforesaid John Shakespeare related above against him..."[5]

John Shakespeare fundamentally contradicted himself in this bill of complaint: on the one hand he admitted that there had been an absolute tranfer of the land, subject only to the unredeemed mortgage proviso (the £40 due on the 29th September, 1580), and on the other he claimed that he was selling outstanding "evidences" for £20. Why should John Lambert agree to the payment of an additional £20 for the surrender of "evidences" when he clearly already owned the land outright? As the author of the Public Record Office pamphlet *Shakespeare In The Public*

Records concluded, John Shakespeare's claim "was dubious in the extreme"[6], and there is no evidence that the case ever reached the courts. A full discussion of the significance of this bill of complaint must wait until we have examined all the evidence in the Shakespeare/Lambert dispute. However, as previously noted, it indicates the speculative, capitalist nature of John Shakespeare's attitude and mentality: that by "buying and bargaining" he expected to be able to make a 50% profit on money invested. Additionally, it links Shakespeare himself into the transaction – suggesting that he was still living in Stratford and working with his father at this late period?

Nine years after John Shakespeare had filed the above complaint, he and his wife submitted (in 1597) an entirely different case against John Lambert, relating to the same land transaction:

> "... [In] consideracion of the somme of fowerty poundes to them by one Edmounde Lamberte . . . your sayde oratours [the Shakespeares] were contente that he, the saide Edmounde Lamberte, shoulde have and enjoye the same premisses untill such tyme as your sayde oratours did repaie unto him the saide somme of fowertie poundes; by reasone whereof the saide Edmounde did enter into the premisses and did occupie the same for the space of three or fower yeares, and the issues and the profyttes thereof did recyve and take; after which your saide oratours did tender unto the said Edmounde the sayde somme of fowerty poundes, and desired that they mighte have againe the sayde premisses accordinge to theire agreement; which money he the sayde Edmounde then refused to receyve, sayinge that he woulde not recyve the same, nor suffer your sayde oratours to have the saide premisses agayne, unlesse they woulde paye unto him certayne other money which they did owe unto him for other matters . . . shortelie after the tendringe of the sayde fowertie poundes to the saide Edmounde, and the desyre of your sayde oratours to have theire lande agayne from him, he the saide Edmounde att Barton aforesayde dyed, after whose deathe one John Lamberte, as sonne and heire of the saide Edmounde, entred into the saide premisses and occupied the same; after which entrie of the sayde John your said oratours came to him and tendred the saide money unto him . . . which he, the saide John, denyed in all thinges, and did withstande them for entringe into the premisses, and as yet doeth so contynewe still ..."[7]

This bill of complaint is totally at odds with the earlier story told by John Shakespeare in 1588: in that year, there was no mention of the repayment of the £40 mortgage, but rather a complaint that John Lambert had refused to pay £20 for further evidence of title; in 1597, the reverse was the case – no mention of non-payment of the £20, but a new claim that the £40 mortgage money had been proffered as stipulated under the original agreement. Paradoxically, John Shakespeare had outlined very clearly in his 1588 complaint the mortgage arrangement on the land: the £40 to be paid by the 29th September 1580, or the land to be forfeited – wheareas in 1597 he merely stated that Edmund Lambert should enjoy the "premisses untill such tyme your sayde oratours did repaie unto him the saide somme of fowertie pounds." And he was extremely vague in his later statement as to when he proffered the £40 in repayment of the mortgage: at one point he said he had offered to pay it "three or fower yeares" after the agreement of 1578, i.e. between 1581 and 1582, and then claimed that "shortelie after the tendringe of the sayde fowertie poundes", Edmund Lambert died – and as the latter died in 1587, this would put the date some five or six years later. And offering the £40 to John Lambert in 1587 would have been irrelevant, given that the mortgage deed clearly stipulated, on John Shakespeare's own admission, payment by 1580. John Lambert's reply to the above complaint was as follows:

> "... [The] said complainante, John Shakespeare, by indenture beringe date uppon or about the fowerteenth daye of November, [1578] . . . for and in consideracion of the summe of fortie powndes of lawfull Englishe monney unto the said complainante paide by Edmunde Lamberte, this defendantes father in the said byll named, did geve, graunte, bargaine and sell the said messuage, and one yearde and fower acres of lande with the appurtenances [in Wilmecott, in the parishe of Aston Cawntloe], unto the said Edmunde Lamberte, and his heires and assignes, to have and to holde the said messuage . . . ; in which indenture there is a condicionall proviso conteyned that, if the said complainante did paye unto the saide Edmunde Lamberte the summe of fortie powndes uppon the feastdaie of St. Michell the Archangel . . . one thousande fyve hundred and eightie, att the dwellinge howse of the said Edmund Lamberte . . . that then the said graunte, bargaine and sale . . . shulde cease and be voyde ... and this defendante further sayeth that the said complainante did not tender or paye the said summe of fortie powndes unto the said Edmunde Lamberte, this defendantes father, uppon the saide feaste daye, which was in the yeare of our Lorde God one thowsande fyve hundred and eightie, accordinge to the said provisoe in the said indenture expressed. By reason whereof this defendantes said father was lawfully and absolutely seized of the said premisses . . . and this defendante further sayeth that the said messuage, yearde lande and other premisses, or the moste part thereof, have ever, sythence the purches therof by this defendantes father, byne in lease by the demise of the said complainante; and the lease thereof beinge now somewhat nere expyred, whereby a greater value is to be yearly raised thereby, they, the said complainantes, doe now trowble and moleste this defendante by unjuste sutes in lawe, thinkinge therby, as yt shoulde seme,

> to wringe from him this defendante some further recompence for the said premisses then they have alreddy received ..."[8]

This statement of John Lambert's confirms the details of the mortgage arrangement outlined by John Shakespeare in 1588: that it was to run for two years until the 29th September 1580, whereupon if not redeemed the land would be transferred absolutely to Edmund Lambert. There is no mention of the £20 for surrender of evidences of title, and this had become an irrelevance inasmuch as the Shakespeares had dropped this contention from their claim in 1597. John Lambert's defence was very straightforward – he stood by the two-year mortgage arrangement earlier conceded by John Shakespeare – and he categorically denied that any payment had been offered to redeem this mortgage. The additional interest of his defence lies in the reference to the lease; although he does not give details of this, he does tell us that it was due to expire soon after 1597, and that there would be a significant increase in its value on renewal. This is almost certainly the lease on the Shakespeare Wilmcote land registered in 1579: it was let out on a peppercorn rent and was due to run out in 1601, but we will return to this lease when presenting a summary analysis of the whole series of transactions centring on the Wilmcote property. In reply to Lambert's defence, John Shakespeare yet again modified his story:

> "... accordinge to the condicion or proviso mencioned in the said indenture of bargaine and sale of the premisses mencioned in the said bill of complaynt, he this complaynant, John Shakespere, did come to the dwellinge-house of the said Edmunde Lambert, in Barton-uppon-the-Heathe, uppon the feaste daie of St.Michaell the archangel . . . one thousand fyve hundred and eightie, and then and there tendered to paie unto him the said Edmunde Lambert the said fortie poundes, which he was to paie for the redempcion of the said premisses; which somme the saide Edmunde did refuse to receyve, sayinge that he owed him other money, and unles that he, the said John, would paie him altogether, as well as the said fortie pounds as the other money, which he owed him over and above, he would not receave the said fortie poundes, and imediatlie after he, the said Edmunde, dyed, and by reason thereof, he, the said defendant, entered into the saide premisses, and wrongfullie kepeth and detayneth the said premisses from him the said complaynant ..."[9]

Again, there is a basic contradiction in this account: on the one hand, John Shakespeare claimed to have proffered the £40 in 1580; on the other, he stated that Edmund Lambert died "immediatlie after" – and as this happened in 1587, there is a discrepancy of something like seven years in the chronology. It is therefore not surprising in the light of all these contradictions and inconsistencies that the case went against John Shakespeare. Although we do not have a formal record of the verdict, it is now known that the land continued in the ownership of the Lambert family; in early 1602, "John Lambert and his Margery his wife sold to Richard Smyth, for forty pounds, forty-six acres of land in Greate Wilmcote, together with two acres of meadow, three acres of pasture, and common of pasture."[10] The case had come full circle: John Shakespeare's lease had come to an end in 1601 – the year of his death – and the Wilmcote land was sold for the same sum for which it was bought – £40. (The Lamberts would have made a small profit on the transaction, as they appear to have retained five of the 56 acres that they acquired in 1578.)

Before analysing the significance of this case, we must take note of two small but interesting additional pieces of evidence on the Shakespeare/Lambert relationship. When Roger Sadler, a baker of Stratford, made his will on the 14th November 1578, he appended to it a list of debts owing to him; one of these was a debt of £5 (£700) owing by "Edmonde Lamberte" and "Edward Cornishe" (another brother-in-law of John Shakespeare), "for the debte of Mr John Shaksper".[11] Lambert was helping his brother-in-law Shakespeare with a loan at the time of the latter's economic difficulties in 1578, and two years later in May, 1580, John Shakespeare's youngest son, Edmund, was christened – and as Halliday has written, he "was probably named after his uncle, Edmund Lambert".[12] All this suggests that the Shakespeares and Lamberts were on very friendly terms until the dispute broke out between them about the Wilmcote property.

We are now in a position to consider the significance of some of the property transactions earlier discussed, in particular the leasing of the Wilmcote land registered in 1579. Given John Shakespeare's economic difficulties in 1578 and his friendly relationship with his brother-in-law, Edmund Lambert, at that time, the most logical explanation of the leasing arrangement is as follows. The lease was divided into two time zones : 1.The period up to the 29th September 1580, when it was leased to Thomas Webbe and Humphrey Hooper. 2.The twenty-one year period from 1580 until 1601 when it was held at a peppercorn rent by George Gibbs as agent for the Shakespeares – an arrangement confirmed by John Lambert's reference to the land being leased "by the demise" of John Shakespeare. This division can only be understood in relation to the mortgage agreement: up until the 29th September 1580, the land was under mortgage to the Lamberts and beyond the control of the

Shakespeares. The latter presumably let the land under lease to Webbe and Hooper either at a full market rent, or had some agreement whereby they could benefit from the income of the farm. The mortgaging and leasing arrangements were structured so that if the Shakespeares were able to redeem the mortgage in 1580, there would be no loss to them, and incidentally no gain to the Lamberts, except for the receipt of the rent from the lease for the period 1578-1580. If they were unable to redeem the mortgage, then the leasing provisions would protect them during the twenty-one year ensuing years: they would have the full income from the farm via their peppercorn/agency arrangement with George Gibbs, in effect a safeguard device as a contingency against not being able to redeem the 1578 mortgage.(It should be noted that only a part of the leased land was mortgaged to the Lamberts – what happened to the other part is not known.)

Whether or not the mortgage was redeemed in 1580, the Lamberts stood to gain very little. They had no access to the income from the land at any point between 1580 and 1601; if the mortgage had been redeemed in 1580, they would have gained nothing – except for the receipt of the rent on the leased land for the two years 1578-1580. In the event, they re-sold the land for the same price as they paid for it twenty-one years after they had acquired title in 1580, although with a very small profit by retaining five acres. All the evidence points to the original mortgage arrangement of 1578 being an act of generosity on the part of Edmund Lambert, designed to help his brother-in-law at a time of difficulty, and this is confirmed by the loan he made (with his fellow brother-in-law, Edward Cornwell/Cornishe) via Roger Sadler in the same year.

What does all this tell us about the conduct and character of John Shakespeare? We are forced to conclude from the evidence that he consistently lied in court about the facts of the case, and was ruthlessly prepared to exploit any weaknesses or possibilities for economic gain. To use his own words, he shewed "scheming and fraudulent intent craftily and cunningly to deceive and defraud" – but the language should be applied to his own conduct, not that of his Lambert relatives. It is presumably because of this that Mary Shakespeare's name was dropped at one stage from the case launched against John Lambert in 1597 [13] – her sister had been married to Edmund Lambert, and this must have put great strains on family loyalties. We can perhaps see the characters of John Shakespeare and John Lambert respectively in the language that they use in ending their submissions: John Shakespeare – "and your sayde oratours shall daylie praye to God for the prosperous healthe of your good lordshippe with increase of honour longe to contynewe"; John Lambert – "All which matters this defendante is reddy to averre and prove, as this honorable courte shall awarde, and prayethe to be dismissed therhence with his reasonable costs and charges in this wrongfull sute by him unjustly sustyeyned."[14] One was the language of flattery and deceit; the other of simplicity and straightforwardness.

John Shakespeare's tactics in dealing with the case can perhaps best be explained by his economic circumstances. In 1588 when he lodged his first bill of complaint, he was near to a point of bankruptcy; Edmund Lambert had just died, and presumably given the complexity of the legal transactions associated with the land, he perhaps felt that he could exploit any uncertainties of title to extract more money from the new heir to the Lambert estate. By 1597 he had returned to prosperity: when he applied for a new coat of arms in 1596, he was said to be worth £500 (this was almost certainly, as we shall see, the result of his son's financial success), and he could now afford to invoke the original mortgage agreement and offer the £40 redemption payment. As John Lambert pointed out, he had a particular incentive to do this as the favourable lease on the land was soon to fall in.

With some confidence, we can now rule out the arguments of Fripp, and Mutschmann & Wentersdorf, about Shakespeare's father suffering economically as a result of religious recusancy; not only is there no direct evidence for this, but the contention put forward by these writers that John Shakespeare had been cheated out of money and property transferred for safekeeping to relatives, such as the Lamberts, collapses completely. We must therefore look elsewhere for the explanation of John Shakespeare's fall.

★ ★ ★

The problems that beset John Shakespeare in the period after 1577 were not confined to economic difficulties and disputes over land ownership. He became embroiled in a number of quarrels and legal entanglements, which have been very succinctly summarized by Schoenbaum :

> "Troubles multiplied. In Trinity term, 1580, John was fined £20 [£2,800] for not appearing in the court of Queen's Bench to find security for keeping the Queen's peace. (At this time the Crown similarly penalized many others,

more than 140 throughout England, with fines of £10 to £200; why is not known.) The same court also fined him another £20 as pledge for a hatmaker of Nottingham [John Audley] who had failed his day to produce surety for good behaviour . . . Evidently John Shakespeare did not always judge well the character of those for whom he vouched. Thus the £10 [£1,400] bail he stood for Michael Price, [a] felonious Stratford tinker, was forfeited. So too was his bond for £10 of a debt of £22 [£3,080] incurred by his brother Henry. On that occasion a suit followed; to escape jail John turned to his friend Alderman Hill for bail, and even swore out a writ of habeas corpus to transfer the case to another court ... Adversaries, as well as adversities, oppressed him. In the summer of 1582 he petitioned for sureties of peace against four men – Ralph Cawdrey, William Russell, Thomas Logginge, and Robert Young – 'for fear of death and mutilation of his limbs'."[15]

Little is known of these friends and associates of John Shakespeare's; John Audley had been fined £10 as a pledge for Shakespeare senior, as had the third member of this circle, Thomas Cooley of Stoke, Staffordshire[16] – and whatever the nature of the original crime, it was clearly very serious involving a breach of the Queen's peace, and incurring a very heavy fine. Michael Price, the tinker, was a near neighbour of John Shakespeare's, but not a great deal is known about him, as is the case with Ralph Cawdrey, William Russell, Thomas Logginge, and Robert Young. More is known about Henry Shakepeare, John Shakespeare's brother, and again we can do no better than quote from Schoenbaum for a summary:

"Henry Shakespeare . . . held land in the Hales manor [Snitterfield], but he also farmed at Ingon in the nearby parish of Hampton Lucy . . . Henry was something of a ne'er-do- well. He got into a fray with one Edward Cornwell (he became the second husband of the poet's Aunt Margaret), drew blood, and was fined, but did not show up in court to answer the charge. He was imprisoned for trespass; he incurred debts and failed to honour them. On one occasion Henry refused to pay his tithe – there was a quarrel between claimants – and for a time suffered excommunication. The authorities fined him for wearing a hat instead of a cap to church: maybe a principle was involved, for many, especially Puritans, resented the Statute of Caps, promulgated to encourage the depressed craft of cappers."[17]

It is a somewhat misleading to call Henry Shakespeare a "ne'er-do-well"; John Shakespeare's chequered history after 1577 reads in similar vein to that of his brother, and generally the Stratford records for the period are littered with references to drunken affrays, fights and personal disputes.[18] Elizabethan society varied so much from our own that we must be wary of applying our own standards of reference, to what in effect was a very different culture. References to dunghills, unmade and pitted roads covered with offal and the remains of slaughtered animals, chickens, pigs and cattle roaming unchecked in the streets, drunken brawls between men wearing knives, daggers and swords – it is easy for the reader of the Stratford documents to believe he has inadvertently stumbled into the "Wild West" – a raw, physical, and violent world.[19] The Stratford Corporation did of course try to control and regulate such excesses, and the records bear out the persistent struggle to subdue these breaches of the puritan code, destined inevitably to fail. The tension and contrast between the puritan style of the corporation and the way of life of the ordinary inhabitants of Stratford was very marked, but this is to anticipate a later argument.

CHAPTER 5: JOHN SHAKESPEARE AS FALSTAFF

A point has now been reached when we must look to William Shakespeare for help in unravelling the enigma of his father. The first clue lies in the list of people not attending church in 1592:

Mr John Wheeler
John Wheeler, his son
Mr John Shakespeare
Mr Nicholas Barnhurst
Thomas James, alias Giles
William Baynton
Richard Harrington
William Fluellen
George Bardolfe

"IT is said that these last nine come not to church for fear of process for debt."[1]

The last two names are familiar – Bardolfe a character out of *Henry IV*, *Henry V*, and *The Merry Wives Of Windsor* – and Fluellen a soldier in *Henry V*. In a supplementary list of recusants for 1592, the name of Court appears – he was also a character out of *Henry V*.[2] It has been generally recognized by Shakespeare historians that these are the most autobiographical of Shakespeare's plays. This is particularly the case with *The Merry Wives Of Windsor*, where the names of Herne, Horne, Brome, Ford, Page, Poins, Peto, Bardolfe and Fenton appear – and these were all people resident in Stratford during Shakespeare's youth.[3] Given that the town only had a population of approximately 1,750 people (about 390 families), this is a most remarkable concentration of local names in one play, suggesting powerful autobiographical associations for Shakespeare. [It is also perhaps no co-incidence that the name of the street at the end of Henley Street is Windsor Street.] Occasionally a single local name appeared in one of his other plays with, as we have seen, the exception of the *Henry IV* and *Henry V* series where there were the four references to Bardolfe, Fluellen, Court and Poins.

Little or nothing is known of the individuals who carried the names of the characters in the plays. The person we know most about is George Bardolfe; he was more commonly known in Stratford as Bardell, and that Shakespeare had him in mind as a model is indicated by the names given to him in the different editions of the plays: Bardoll, Bardolfe and Bardolph. By trade Bardolfe/Bardell was a mercer and a grocer and had been nominated as a burgess of Stratford corporation in 1580 (he had previously been a constable). He was elected chamberlain in 1582 but was excused from serving for reasons unstated but accepted by the corporation. He was elected alderman in 1584 but does not appear to have taken up his position, as he continued to be listed as a burgess. He acted as one of the chamberlains in 1586, but from 1588 ceased attending corporation meetings and was struck off the list of burgesses (for non-attendance) on the 14th August 1590.

Writs of arrest were issued against Bardell for debt in 1588 and 1592, and he was imprisoned in the latter year; according to Eccles "the under-sheriff of Warwickshire, Basil Trymnell, at first let Bardell drink in a tavern in Warwick but when warned that he might escape kept him 'in a more Strayter manner' and secured him by 'a Locke with a Longe yron Chayne and a greate clogge."[4] Bardell's debts were apparently partly due to the indebtedness of his partner Charles Baynton, but his withdrawal from corporation meetings may have been of his own making. What we know of Bardell/Bardolfe is consistent with Shakespeare's use of him as a model for the comical character Bardoll/Bardolfe/Bardolph. Practically nothing is known about Fluellen, the other person listed with John Shakespeare and George Bardolfe in 1592. His widow, like George Bardell's, was admitted in 1604 to the Stratford almhouse on grounds of poverty.[5]

★ ★ ★

All the relevant aspects of the biographical background have now been covered, and we are in a position to state the central thesis of this section of the book. The major clue to unravelling John Shakeapeare's enigma lies in the only contemporary description of him. As we have seen, in about 1657, Thomas Plume, wrote about Shakespeare : "He was a glovers son – Sir John Mennis saw once his old Father in his shop – a merry Cheekd old man – that said – Will was a good Honest Fellow, but he durst have crackt a jeast with him at any time."[6]

Where do we find such a figure, "merry-cheeked", jesting, a man of good humour? A key is found partly in John Shakespeare's family name – his father, Richard Shakespeare, is listed in one class of records as having the surname of Shakstaff[7] – giving Shakespeare's father the name of *John Shakstaff*. The other clues have already been laid: the appearance on a list with Bardolfe and Fluellen; the impoverished man, acting "with scheming and fraudulent intent, craftily and cunningly to deceive and defraud"; the Protestant who had fallen out of grace; but above all the man who dominates Shakespeare's autobiographical plays, *The Merry Wives Of Windsor*, *1, Henry IV*, and *2, HenryIV:* Such a man is **John Falstaff.**

★ ★ ★

The poet, W.H.Auden, saw perhaps more clearly than anyone else the paradox of Falstaff's position in the *Henry IV* plays; he wrote:

> "What sort of bad company would one expect to find Prince Hal keeping when the curtain rises on *Henry IV?* Surely, one could expect to see him surrounded by daring, rather sinister juvenile delinquents and beautiful gold-digging whores. But whom do we meet in the Boar's Head? A fat, cowardly tosspot, old enough to be his father, two down-at-heel hangers-on, a slatterny hostess and only one whore, who is not in her earliest youth either; all of them seedy, and, by any worldly standards, including those of the criminal classes, all of them *failures*. Surely, one thinks, an Heir Apparent, sowing his wild oats, could have picked himself a more exciting crew than that. As the play proceeds, our surprise is replaced by another kind of puzzle, for the better we come to know Falstaff, the clearer it becomes that the world of historical reality which a Chronicle Play claims to imitate is not a world which he can inhabit."[8]

There is virtually no literary or historical basis for the character of Falstaff, although the character may have been partly based on the Lollard, Sir John Oldcastle, who appeared briefly (he had a few lines) in the source play, *The Famous Victories Of Henry V*. Shakespeare made a play on Oldcastle's name in the epilogue of *2, Henry IV*, and there were a number of survivals of the name in the text. According to contemporary sources, Shakespeare changed the name of Oldcastle to Falstaff as a result of political pressure from Oldcastle's influential descendants. Shakespeare also probably changed the name because of the existence of a Protestant contemporary of Oldcastle, Sir John Falstolfe – and he wanted a figure with a strong puritan/protestant background for the creation of the Falstaff character.

Although cast in comical form the *Henry IV* plays bear out Falstaff's Protestant history; in *1, Henry IV* (Act 1, Scene 2) Falstaff says to Hal: "O, thou hast damanable iteration, and art indeede able to corrupt a Saint . . . Before I knew thee *Hal*, I knew nothing: and now I am (if a man shold speake truly) little better then one of the wicked. I must giue ouer this life, and I will giue it over." To which Hal jokingly replies: "I see a good amendment of life in thee: From Praying, to Purse taking." Likewise, in 2, iv, Hal says: "Now my Masters, for a true Face, and good Conscience" – to which, Falstaff rejoins: "Both of which I haue had, but their date is out..." In 3, iii, Falstaff confesses: "Do'st thou heare *Hal?* Thou know'st in the state of Innocency, *Adam* fell: and what should poor *Jacke Falstaffe* do, in the dayes of Villany? . . . Well, Ile repent, and that suddenly, while I am in some liking: I shall be out of heart shortly, and then I shall haue no strength to repent. And I haue not forgotten what the in-side of a Church is made of."

That this plea for repentence is not just a comical device, is indicated in the other Falstaff plays. In *2, Henry IV* (2, ii) Falstaff tells Pistol: "I, I , I myself sometimes, leaving the fear of God on the left hand and hiding my honour in my necessity, am fain to shuffle, to hedge, and to lurch ..." And in *The Merry Wives Of Windsor* (4, v) he confesses: "I neuer prosper'd, since I foreswore my selfe at *Primero:* well, if my winde were but long enough; I would repent." His reputation is that of an honourable man: Page tells Ford that "the Priest o' th' Towne commended him for a true man", to which Ford rejoins, "T'was a good sensible fellow". (2, i). This is echoed by Mrs Ford, who confirms Falstaff's respectable past: "hee would not sweare: praise womens modesty: and gaue such orderly and wel-behaued reproofe to all vncomelinesse, that I would haue sworne his disposition would haue gone to the truth of his words." (1, iv) His bed is "painted about with the story of the Prodigall, fresh and new" (4, v), and in *Henry V* (2, ii), as he dies, he cries "out, God, God, God".

Falstaff is a failure by worldly standards: in *The Merry Wives of Windsor* (1, iii), he confesses that he is "almost out at heeles", and is described "as poore as Job" (5, v). At the end of the play, Ford tells us that "twenty pounds of money . . . must be paid [by Falstaff] to Mr *Broome* [for which] his horses are arrested . . . [and] to repay that money will be a biting affliction." (5, v) In *2, Henry IV* (1, ii) he is again "as poore as *Job* . . . but not so Patient": "I can get no remedy against this Consumption of the purse. Borrowing onely lingers, and lingers it out, but the disease is incureable." After picking Falstaff's pocket – and finding there a list of "one halfe penny-worth of Bread to this intollerable deale of Sacke" – Hal asks Falstaff what he has lost. Falstaff replies: "Whilst thou beliue me, *Hal?* Three or four Bonds of fortie pound apeece, and a Seale-Ring of my Grandfathers." (*1, Henry IV*, 3, iii). The point of the rejoinder is of course to bring out the comic discrepancy between the reality of Falstaff's dissolute poverty, and his claims to financial standing – but the possession of "three or four Bonds of fortie pound apiece" is more appropriate to John Shakespeare's occupation as an individual trader, than to Falstaff's world of broken-down knight.

Falstaff looks to Prince Hal for financial rescue: "[He] sayde this other day, You [the Prince] ought him a thousand pound." (*1, Henry IV*, 3, iii). Falstaff is preoccupied with obtaining this sum of £1,000: when challenged about his cowardice, he tells the prince that "I would giue a thousand pound I could run as fast as thou canst . . . here be foure of vs, haue ta'ne a thousand pound this Morning" (*1, Henry IV*, 2, iv). He asks the Lord Chief Justice: "Will your Lordship lend mee a thousand pound, to furnish me forth" (*2, Henry IV*, 1, ii), and eventually persuades the gullible Shallow to lend him the thousand pounds in anticipation of the fruits of Prince Hal's succession to the throne (*2, Henry IV*, 5, v). Although Falstaff is disappointed in Hal's reaction to him, the new king does promise him that "competence of life, I will allow you,/ That lack of meanes enforce you not to euill:/ And as we heare you do reforme your selues,/ We will according to your strength, and qualities,/ Give you aduancement." (*2, Henry IV*, 5, v).

Falstaff's lapsed Protestantism and acute poverty are exact parallels to John Shakespeare's condition and situation in the mid-1590's, when Shakespeare began writing the *Henry IV* plays. The parallel goes further: Rowe in his biography states that "my Lord Southampton, at one time, gave him [Shakespeare] a thousand Pounds, to enable him to go through with a Purchase he had a mind to"[9]; and R.B. Wheeler in his *History And Antiquities Of Stratford-Upon-Avon*, published in 1806, tells us that "the unanimous tradition of this neighbourhood is that by the uncommon bounty of the Earl of Southampton, he [Shakespeare] was enabled to purchase houses and land in Stratford."[10] Shakespeare bought New Place in 4 May 1597, but more importantly, his father's fortunes had been restored sufficiently by 1596 for him to claim when applying for a coat of arms, "that he hath Landes and tenementes of good wealth, & substance £500."[11]

Falstaff shows some sensitivity to his status as a gentleman: at one point in *2, Henry IV*, he exclaims, "As I am a Gentleman", and is rebuked by Mistress Quickly – "Nay, you said so before" – to which Falstaff rejoins again, "As I am a Gentleman."[12] John Shakespeare likewise was concerned to establish his claims to gentility: when applying for his coat of arms, he stated that he "hath maryed the daughter (& one of the heyres of Robert Arden of Wilmcoote in the said) Counte esquire", and that his "parent great Grandfather and late Antecessor, for his faithefull & approved service to the late most prudent prince king H 7 of famous memorie, was advuanced & rewarded with Landes & Tenementes geven to him in those partes of Warwikeshere where they have continewed bie some decentes in good reputacon & credit."[13] Chambers has questioned the validity of these claims, and concluded that "the landed status of the early Warwickshire Shakespeares, so far as discoverable, was that of manorial copyholders, or at the very most freeholders or leaseholders"; and that Robert Arden had never been styled esquire or gentleman – in fact, he was almost certainly a mere "husbandman".[14] Although exaggerated claims were common in the applications for coats of arms, the degree and extent of John Shakespeare's exaggerations are entirely compatible with his identification with Falstaff.

There are echoes of Falstaff in the character of the shepherd in *The Winter's Tale*. The shepherd and his son, the clown, are to be rewarded for having inadvertently adopted Perdita, daughter of Leontes, King of Sicily – and as a result, are anticipating gentleman status:

> "*Shepherd* Come Boy, I am past moe Children: but thy Sonnes and Daughters will be all Gentlemen borne.
> *Clown* You are well met (Sir:) you deny'd to fight with mee this other day, because I was no Gentleman borne . . . now I am a Gentleman? Let Boores and Franklins say it, Ile sweare it.
> *Shepherd* How if it be false (Sonne?)
> *Clown* If it be ne'er so false, a true Gentleman may sweare it, in the behalfe of his Friend. And Ile sweare to the Prince, thou art a tall Fellow of thy hands, and that thou wilt not be drunke: but I know that thou art no tall Fellow of thy hands and that thou wilt be drunke." (5, ii)

At about the time that Shakespeare was writing the Falstaff plays, his friend and rival, Ben Jonson, wrote what many consider satirical references to the Shakespeare application for a coat of arms. Schoenbaum has summarized the episode as follows: "In his *Poetaster* Jonson sneers at common players who aspire to heraldic distinctions . . . and some have seen mockery of Shakespeare's motto in *Every Man Out Of*

His Humour, in which the rustic clown Sogliardo, fresh from having laid out £30 for his arms, is mocked with the words, 'Not without mustard'.[The Shakespeares' motto was, 'Not without right'.] The parallel is suggestive, but Sogliardo is not an actor, and his coat-armour, which flaunts a boar's head, is unlike Shakespeare's."[15] *But the coat of arms was not applied for by William but by John Shakespeare – and although Sogliardo is not an actor, he is a rustic clown – and his coat armour is a "boar's head"*. What more effective way of satirizing John Shakespeare as Falstaff could Jonson have devised? – and Jonson is likely to have known the relevant background, as he was a friend of Shakespeare's, and according to one contemporary source, had visited Shakespeare in Stratford.[16] Also, Shakespeare probably satirized Jonson in the character of Nym – whose frequent exclamations of "by my humour" refer to Jonson's own satirical plays – suggesting a mild satirical battle between the two playwrights. However, it should be pointed out that Jonson's satire was for a public audience, and that any private allusions would be secondary; "Not Without Mustard", had originated with Thomas Nashe in his *Pierce Penilesse*[17], and presumably Jonson was, at least in part, making satirical reference to this.

There are references in *1, Henry IV* which can be read directly as linking John Shakespeare to Falstaff. In Act 2, Scene 4, Falstaff says "When I was about thy yeeres (*Hal*) I was not an Eagles Talent in the Waste, I could haue crept into any Aldermans Thumbe-Ring" – and as John Shakespeare was in his thirties when he was appointed an Alderman, and Shakespeare was the same age when he wrote this play, the potential association is clear.

Falstaff's relationship to Hal is that of father to son: "Thou art my Sonne: I haue partly thy Mothers Word, partly my Opinion; but chiefly, a villanous tricke of thine Eye, and a foolish hanging of thy nether Lippe, that doth warrant me. If then thou be Sonne to mee, heere lyeth the point: why, being Sonne to me, art thou so poynted at? Shall the blessed Sonne of Heauan proue a Micher, and eate Black-berryes?" (*1, Henry IV*, 2, iv) Elsewhere, Hal refers to Falstaff as "that Father Ruffian", whose "Lyes are like the Father that begets them."[18] Falstaff in turn boasts of his influence over his adopted son: "Hereof comes it, that Prince *Harry* is valiant: for the cold blood hee did naturally inherite of his Father, hee hath, like leane, stirrill, and bare Land, manured, husbanded, and tyll'd, with excellent endeauour of drinking good, and good store of fertile Sherris, that he is become very hot, and valiant. If I had a thousand Sonnes, the first Principle I would teach them, should be to foreswore thinne Potations, and to addict themselues to Sack."[19] And Shakespeare brings this relationship into even more explicit focus in the fourth scene of Act 2 of *1, Henry IV*:

> "*Prince* Doe thou stand for my Father, and examine mee vpon the particulars of my Life.
> *Falstaff* Shall I? content: This Chayre shall bee my State, this Dagger my Scepter, and this Cushion my Crowne.
> *Prince* Thy State is taken for a Joyn'd-Stoole, thy Golden Scepter for a Leaden Dagger, and thy precious rich Crowne, for a pittifull bald Crowne."

The whole tone of the relationship between Falstaff and Hal is similar to that of John Shakespeare with his son: "Will was a good honest fellow, but he durst have crackt a jeast with him at any time." There are echoes of this relationship also in other plays: in *The Comedy Of Errors* (1, ii), Antipholus describes Dromio as "A trustie villiane sir, that very oft,/ When I am dull with care and melancholly,/ Lightens my humour with his merry jests." And likewise, in *The Merchant Of Venice* (1, i), Gratiano disclaims: "Let me play the foole,/ With mirth and laughter let old wrinkles come/ And let my Liuer rather heat with wine." Sonnets 45 and 50 suggest that Shakespeare was often in need of such merriment, particularly after a long journey: "How heavy do I journey on the way . . . The beast that bears me, tired with my woe . . . oppress'd with melancholy."

Although Hal is the hero of the *Henry IV* and *Henry V* plays, he takes on a number of 'low' disguises which have no bearing on the main narrative plot of the plays. At the end of the second scene, act two of *2, Henry IV*, in order to spy on Falstaff, Poins suggests that he and Hal "Put on two Leather Jerkins, and Aprons, and waite vpon him at his Table, like Drawers" – to which Hal rejoins: "From Prince, to a Prentice, a low transformation, that shall be mine" – the apprentice-like relationship between Hal and Falstaff mirroring the actual relationship between John Shakespeare and his son. A similar but more revealing 'low' transformation occurs in *Henry V:* Hal, now King Henry V, meets a soldier Williams (companion to Court, whose name appeared in the 1592 recusancy list), and sets in train a series of minor incidents totally irrelevant to the main plot of the play.

The king is acting *incognito* on the battlefield, and enters into a mock-quarrel with Williams; they agree to exchange gloves, to be worn in their caps, as gages of recognition for a future encounter. The king subsequently persuades Fluellen to wear Williams's glove, tricking him into believing that it is the emblem of one of their French enemies, who he instructs Fluellen to capture. When apprehended, Williams protests to the king: "Your Majestie came not like your selfe: you appear'd to me but as a common man; witnesse the Night, your Garments, your Lowlinesse: and what your Highnesse suffer'd vnder that shape."[20]

This incident then becomes shuffled into a symbolic association with the wearing of leeks by the Welsh soldiers present in the battle, one of whom is Fluellen. The latter reminds the king of this tradition: "If your Majesties is remembred of it, the Welchmen did good seruice in a Garden where Leekes did grow, wearing Leekes in their *Monmouth* caps, which your Maiesty know to this houre is an honourable badge of the seruice: And I do beleeue your Maiesty takes no scorne to weare the Leeke vppon S.Tauies day" – to which the king replies, "I weare it for a memorable honor: For I am Welch you know good Countriman."[21] And almost immediately afterwards, the king encounters Williams wearing his glove in his cap, and sets in train his capture by Fluellen. Earlier in the same scene, Fluellen draws a parallel between Alexander the Great and Henry V – and semi-humorously puts down Alexander – calling him Alexander the pig – in order elevate his king, Harry of Monmouth. He also reminds his audience that "as *Alexander* kild his friend *Clytus*, being in his Ales and his Cuppes; so also *Harry Monmouth* being in his right wittes, and his good judgements, turn'd away the fat Knight [Sir John Falstaffe]." Shakespeare develops this theme by engineering a quarrel between Fluellen and Pistol (who is a surrogate character for Falstaff) – resulting in Pistol being forced to eat the leek that Fluellen wears in his cap.[22]

This complicated and somewhat contorted series of events – humorously inappropriate for the context – is wholly characteristic of Shakespeare when he is exploring themes not directly relevant to the narrative structure of the play, but which have personal significance. There is a 'low' transformation in this series of events, equivalent to the "prince to prentice" incident, but with the additional significance that the 'low' emblem that Hal identifies himself with is – *a glove*. And through the symbolism of the leek/glove, the apparent nobility of the Welsh Tudor dynasty is reduced to the biographical world of Falstaff and the glover, John Shakespeare. Not only is Pistol humiliated through the eating of Fluellen's leek, but Falstaff is symbolically killed off by Alexander the pig/Harry of Monmouth.

The killing off of Falstaff is associated with the hunting of deer, described in *The Merry Wives Of Windsor*, and referred to indirectly in the other autobiographical plays. Shakespeare was caught and punished for poaching Sir Thomas Lucy's deer – this is a theme which will be dealt with at length later – and there is evidence that Shakespeare satirized Lucy in the form of Justice Shallow. In *The Merry Wives Of Windsor*, Shallow accuses Falstaff: "Knight, you haue beaten my men, kill'd my deere, and broke open my Lodge" (Act 1, Scene 1, Folio Edition – in the Quarto Edition this becomes, "Sir John, Sir John, you have hurt my keeper, kild my dogs, stolne my deere.") Master Page, father of young William, entertains Falstaff to venison pasty as the play opens – and inadvertently exacerbates Shallow's injuries by thanking him for a present of the venison, which has actually been poached by Falstaff.

In Shakespeare's mind, there was an indelible link between Falstaff and deer: in *The Merry Wives Of Windsor* Falstaff is pursued and hunted – he refers to himself as "a Windsor Stagge", is called "my Deere", "My male-Deere" by Mrs Ford, and confesses of himself that "when night dogs run, all sorts of deer are chased" – and in the final scene enters disguised as Herne "with a buck's head upon him". In *2, Henry IV*, when Prince Hal discovers Falstaff apparently dead, he exclaims: "Deathe hath not strucke so fat a Deere today" (5, iv), and in the epilogue to the play, Shakespeare promises his audience that "if you be not too much cloid with Fat Meate, our humble Author will continue the Story (with Sir John in it)." Falstaff's attempt to cuckold Ford and Page redounds against him, and he is justly punished by being made to wear horns. Shakespeare interweaves the theme of the hunting of Falstaff with his rejection by Prince Hal. In the Quarto version of *The Merry Wives Of Windsor*, as Falstaff begins to discover how he has been tricked into dressing as a buck-deer, he is made to say: "What hunting at this time of night? Ile lay my life the mad Prince of Wales/ Is stealing his fathers Deare." We see here a direct link between Shakespeare's own poaching activities and those of Prince Hal, but in the context of his rejection of wildness, embodied in the figure of Falstaff, who is hunted and eventually killed off.

Hal's wildness as a young man is described in the appropriate historical plays. In *Richard II* (5, iii), Bolingbroke complains of his son's behaviour: "Can no man tell me of my vnthriftie Sonne?/ 'Tis full three monthes since I did see him last . . . Enquire at London, 'mongst the Tauernes there:/ For there (they say), he dayly doth frequent,/ With vnrestrained loose Companions . . . " In *2, Henry IV* (4, v), Bolingbroke (now king), reiterates this complaint: "For the Fift *Harry*, from curb'd License pluckes/ The muzzle of Restraint; and the wilde Dogge/ Shall flesh his tooth in euery innocent." He cross-examines Prince Humphrey and Prince Clarence, Hal's brothers, on the latter's whereabouts:

> "*King* . . . where is the Prince, your Brother?
> *Prince Humphrey* I thinke hee's gone to hunt (my Lord) at Windsor...
> *King* And how accompanyed? Canst thou tell that?
> *Prince Clarence* With *Pointz,* and other his continuall followers.
> *King* . . . when his head-strong Riot hath no Curbe,/ When Rage and hot-Blood are his Counsailors,/ When Meanes and lauish Manners meete together;/ Oh, with what Wings shall his Affections flye/ Towards fronting Perill, and oppos'd Decay?" (4, iv)

This speech foreshadows Hal's abandonment of his "wild youth", and Warwick predicts that the "Prince will, in the perfectnesse of time,/ Cast off his followers: and their memorie/ Shall as a Patterne, or a Measure, liue . . . Turning past euils to advantages." (4, iv) Hal's transformation is described in *Henry V* (1, i):

> "... his addiction was to Courses vaine,/ His Companies vnletter'd, rude, and shallow,/ His Houres fill'd vp with Ryots, Banquets, Sports;/ And neuer noted in him any studie,/ Any retyrement, any sequestration/ From open Haunts and Popularitie . . . The breath no sooner left his Fathers body/ But that his wildnesse, mortify'd in him,/ Seem'd to dye too: yea, at that very moment,/ Consideration like an Angel came/ And whipt th'offending *Adam* out of him . . . Neuer was such a sodaine Scholler made:/ Neuer came Reformation in a Flood ..."

This is associated with Hal's rejection of Falstaff, the misleader of youth, a figure that represents all that is dissolute, disorderly and wild. But he is more than an abstract "lord of misrule" – his relationship with Hal is highly personal, and although essentially a comic character, at the end he becomes something of a tragic figure, albeit in absurd form. His rejection is foreshadowed in act two, scene four of *1, Henry IV*, where Falstaff playfully says, in the third person, to Hal: "banish not him thy *Harryes* companie, banish not him thy *Harryes* companie; banish plumpe *Jacke*, and banish all the World." The actual rejection occurs at the end of *2, Henry IV:*

> "*Falstaff* But to stand stained with Trauaile, and sweating with desire to see him, thinking of nothing else, putting all affayres in obliuion, as if there were nothing els to bee done, but to see him ...
>
> *Enter King Henrie the Fifth, Brothers, Lord Chief Justice.*

> *Falstaff* Save thy Grace, King *Hall*, my Royall *Hall* ...
> *King* My Lord Chiefe Justice, speake to that vaine man.
> *Chief Justice* Haue you your wits? Know you what 'tis you speake?
> *Falstaff* My King! my Joue! I speake to thee, my heart.
> *King* I know thee not, old man: Fall to thy Prayers:/ How ill white haires become a Foole, and Jester?/ I haue long dream'd of such a kinde of man,/ So surfeit-swell'd, so old, and so profane:/ But, being awake, I do despise my dreame./ Make less thy body (hence) and more thy Grace,/ Leaue gormandizing; Know the Graue doth gape/ For thee, thrice wider then for other men."[23]

There is something very moving about this rejection, and it is anything but comical. Falstaff uses the language of love: "sweating with desire to see him . . . I speake to thee, my heart"; Hal's rejection, although justified by his position and situation, is one of cruelty, and the reader's sympathy cannot but be with Falstaff. Shakespeare makes it abundantly clear that this is no superficial or ephemeral relationship: the scene above is charged with a great intensity of feeling. The jesting and humour fall away to reveal a deeply serious relationship; the rejection of Falstaff culminates in his death – as he is about to die, the hostess tells his followers: "the King has kild his heart."[24]

The elimination of Falstaff at this stage of the play has always been something of a puzzle. In the epilogue of *2, Henry IV*, Shakespeare states his intention of using Falstaff in the sequel, *Henry V*, and there is no obvious reason why he should eliminate such an outstandingly successful comic character. A clue to the solution of this puzzle lies in the repentance shown by Falstaff as he dies – crying out "God, God, God". Falstaff's repentance is mirrored by the shift in John Shakespeare's attitude to religion during the period that these plays were written. In 1595 Shakespeare's father bought a book from a collection of four, the other three of which are known to have been prayer-books.[25] At some point between his non- attendance at church in 1592 and his leaving a Catholic religious will in about 1601, John Shakespeare was converted to Catholicism. The association between Falstaff and John Shakespeare explains the elimination of Falstaff from *Henry V:* at about the time the play was written (it was first published in 1599), John Shakespeare was undergoing a religious conversion that made him no longer a suitable subject for satire. It is not too fanciful to imagine that as he neared death, Shakespeare's father was afflicted with the kind of illness attributed to Falstaff at his end – changes which radically affected Shakespeare's attitude towards his comic creation.

CHAPTER 6:
THE FALL OF JOHN SHAKESPEARE

We are now in a position to address ourselves directly to the question posed at the beginning of this book: what is the explanation for John Shakespeare's fall from prosperity and status in the 1570's? Falstaff hints at a solution to this riddle in act two, scene two of *1, Henry IV*. He complains of Poins: "I am accurst to rob in that Theefe company . . . I haue forsworn his company hourley any time this two and twenty yeare, & yet I am bewitcht with the Rogues company. If the Rascall haue not given me medicines to make me loue him, Ile behang'd; it could not be else: I have drunke Medicines . . . And 'twere not as good a deed as to drinke to turne True- man ..." The first quarto of *2, Henry IV* was published in 1598 – "two and twenty years" previous to this takes us back to 1576, the year in which the dramatic deterioration in John Shakespeare's fortunes took place. There was a Master Poins living in the Stratford area at that time, although virtually nothing is known about him.[1] However, the importance of this passage is that it points us in the direction of an explanation of John Shakespeare's fall.

That Falstaff is virtually synonymous with drink and riotous living is commonplace; his addiction to sack is reflected in a long monologue extolling the virtues of alcohol: "A good Sherris-Sack hath a two-fold operation in it: it ascends me into the Braine, dryes me there all the foolish, and dull, and crudie Vapours, which enuiron it: makes it aprehensiue, quicke, forgetiue, full of nimble, fierie, and delectable shapes; which deliuered o're to the Voyce, the Tongue, which is the Birth, becomes excellent Wit. The second propertie of your excellent Sherris, is, the warming of the Blood; which before (cold and settled) left the Liuer white, and pale ..." (*2, Henry IV*, 4, iii).

There are echoes of Falstaff's character in a number of other plays; Christopher Sly in *The Taming Of The Shrew* is addicted to drink, and although heavily satirized – there are suggestions of the Lambert family: "Am I not Christopher Sly, old Sly's son of Burton Heath ...?" – there are hints that he too once had led a sober life: "Oh how we joy to see your wit restor'd/ Oh that once more you knew but what you are:/ These fifteene yeeres you haue bin in a dreame." (Induction, ii). Sir Toby Belch in *Twelth Night*, is perhaps the character nearest to Falstaff, but not only is he a minor figure, he lacks the substance and depth, and does not come alive in the way that Falstaff does. The question of drink and drunkeness is explored very widely by Shakespeare in a number of the plays – for example, *2, Henry VI*, 2, iv, *Anthony And Cleopatra*, 2, vii, and *The Tempest*, 2, ii – but none of these, or the passages already quoted from *Henry IV*, do justice to a change which was as dramatic as that which took place in John Shakespeare's life. This would reverberate much more powerfully in his son's writings, and indeed we find just such a potent reverberation:

"*HAMLET, Act 1, Scene 4.*

Hamlet The ayre bites shroudly, it is very colde.
Horatio It is a nipping, and an eager ayre.
Hamlet What houre now?
Horatio I thinke it lackes of twelfe.
Marcellus No, it is strooke.
Horatio Indeede; I heard it not, it then drawes neere the season,/ Wherein the spirit held his wont to walke.
(*A florish of trumpets and 2 peeces goes of.*)
What does this meane my Lord?
Hamlet The King doth wake to night and takes his rowse./ Keepes wassell and the swaggring vp-spring reeles:/ And as he draines his drafts of Rhennish downe,/ The kettle drumme, and trumpet, thus bray out/ The triumph of his pledge.
Horatio Is it a custome?
Hamlet I marry ist/ But to my minde, though I am natiue heere/ And to the manner borne, it is a custome/ More honoured in the breach, then the obseruance./ This heavy headed reueale east and west/ Makes vs tradust, and taxed of other nations,/ They clip vs drunkards, and with Swinish phrase/ Soyle our addition, and indeede it takes/ From our achieuements, though perform'd at height/ The pith and marrow of our attribute,/ So oft it chaunces in particuler men,/ That for some vicious mole of nature in them/ As in their birth wherein they are not guilty,/ (Since nature cannot choose his origin)/ By their ore-grow'th of some complextion/ Oft breaking downe the pales and forts of reason,/ Or by some habit, that too much ore-leauens/ The forme of plausiue manners, that these men/ Carrying I say the stamp of one defect/ Being Natures liuery, or Fortunes starre,/ His vertues els be they as pure as grace,/ As infinite as man may vndergoe,/ Shall in the

generall censure take corruption/ From that particular fault : the dram of eale/ Doth all the noble substance of a doubt/ To his own scandle.

Enter Ghost."[2]

The solution to the enigma of John Shakespeare's fall is revealed in this passage: "This heauy headed reueale east and west/ Makes vs tradust, and taxed of other nations,/ They clip vs drunkards, and with Swinish phrase/ Soyle our addition, and indeede it takes/ From our achieuements, though perform'd at height." Due to alcoholism, John Shakespeare fell in economic and social status, even though he had reached a pinnacle of success in 1576. The result was a stigma with traumatic impact on Shakespeare; much of his determination to succeed derived from a reaction to this failure. The rejection of Falstaff is a symbolic representation of the turning away from the world of John Shakespeare, with all its failure and social humiliation. The experience influenced his work, not only through the autobiographical plays which involved the Falstaff/ John Shakespeare connection, but also through the later, more tragic writing, particularly *Hamlet.*

This writing was not of course merely a reflection of autobiographical experience. Jenkins has pointed out that the passage quoted above from *Hamlet* was heavily influenced by Nashe's *Pierce Penniless*, which describes the Danes as "bursten-bellied sots", refers to "the quick-witted Italians . . . [who] detest this *swinish* generation", and categorizes the reveller at home in contrast to the reveller abroad as "the *heavy-headed* gluttonous house-dove."[3] He goes on to cite a passage which has many similarities to the one in *Hamlet;* referring to drunkeness, Nashe tells us

> "A mightie deformer of mens manners and features, is this vnnecessary vice of all other. Let him be indued with neuer so many vertues, and haue as many goodly proportion and faucr as nature can bestow vppon man: yet if hee be thirstie after his own destruction, and hath no ioy nor comfort, but when he drowning his soul in a gallon pot, that one beastly imperfection will vtterlie obscure all that is commendable in him; and all his good qualities sinke like lead down to the bottome of his carrowsing cups, where they will lie, like lees and dregges, dead and vnregarded of any man."[4]

Undoubtedly, Shakespeare was influenced by this passage, as well as the other references to drunkenness in Nashe's work. But the above passage refers to the behaviour of Englishmen, and drunkenness is singled out as one of their most prevalent vices. Shakespeare himself confirms the reputation of Englishmen for drunkenness through one of Iago's speeches – referring to a song he has just sung: "I learn'd it in

England: where indeed they are most potent in Potting. Your Dane, your Germaine, and your swag-belly'd Hollander, (drinke hoa) are nothing to your English . . . Why, he drinkes you with facillitie, your Dane dead drunke. He sweates not to ouerthrow your Almaine; he giues your Hollander a vomit, ere the next Pottle can be fill'd."[5]

There is no incompatibility between Nashe's influence on Shakespeare, and the autobiographical nature of the passage about drunkenness in *Hamlet*. "Perception is functionally selective", and material which has strong personal resonance, is likely for that reason, to be remembered and used at a later date. But this raises the question as to what led John Shakespeare to turn to drink in such disastrous fashion in 1576? A clue to the answer might lie in *The Rape Of Lucrece;* discussing Tarquin's motivation, Shakespeare tells us:

> "Those that much covet are with gain so fond/ That what they have not, that which they possess/ They scatter and unloose it from their bond,/ And so, by hoping more, the profit of excess/ Is but to surfeit, and such griefs sustain/ That they prove bankrupt in this poor-rich gain ... So that in vent'ring ill we leave to be/ The things we are for that which we expect;/ And this ambitious foul infirmity,/ In having much, torments us with defect/ Of that we have; so then we do neglect/ The thing we have and, all for want of wit,/ Make something nothing by augmenting it."[6]

Shakespeare reveals more about the loss of money and wealth in *Timon Of Athens;* Timon's loyal steward Flavius, tells us how Timon has become bankrupt: "When all our Offices hauve been oppresst/ With riotous Feeders, when our Vaults haue wept/ With drunken spilth of Wine, when euery roome/ Hath blaz'd with Lights, and braid with Minstrelsie,/ I have retyr'd me to a wastefull cocke/ And set mine eyes at flow."[7] Flavious elaborates on this theme in a further speech: "No care, no stop, so senselesse of expence/ That he will neither know how to maintaine it/ Nor cease his flow of Riot."[8] The language of riot pervades the accounts of Timon's fall – and the counter-pointing between surfeit, excess and reaction is a strong part of Timon's fate. There is something in the excess of Timon that is reminscent of Falstaff – "so surfeit swelled": his genorosity, his "drunken spilth of wine", and "minstrelsie." And as Shakespeare knew, the reaction of the puritan to the frustrations of constraint led to "gravity's revolt to wantoness". Although there is evidence that like Tarquin, John Shakespeare did "prove bankrupt in this poor-rich gain", there was a suddenness in his fall that requires special explanation. Part of the explanation probably lies in his life as an individual trader. Everitt has described the dangers and vulnerabilities that traders were particularly suseptible to, and this is so central, that it will be quoted fully:

> "There were no banks, and a man's 'credit' could only be what he was taken to be worth in his local community. The very word 'credit' was synonymous with a man's 'estate', 'worth', or 'standing' in local society; but when factors and drovers were travelling all over the country such a conception became nugatory. It was only through the highly personal links of the wayfaring community that it retained any meaning. The problem was really twofold. First, there was a strong temptation for those with much address or little acumen to engage in dealings beyond their means or worth. All went well till some customer defaulted or the harvest failed; then disaster ensued, perhaps involving a score of other victims, unaware of their client's shaky status when they dealt with him. Secondly, there was the temptation to inflict injury on the credit of one's opponent. The dread of 'losing reputation' was not simply a fear of losing caste. It might mean the end of one's business and the impoverishment of one's family. When a wool dealer of Warwick caused his former partner John Lee, glover, 'to be arrested in Cirencester in the county of Gloucester in the open market there, where (Lee's) most credit was, by writ of *capias ad satisfaciend*,' that partner found himself greatly damnified and 'almost utterly undone'. The reputation of Humphrie Grigg of Beaudesert in Warwickshire, as a result of 'unlawful and unconscionable proceedings' of Robert Wheeler of Tanworth in Arden, was 'called into question and his estate descanted upon, so far as whereas before such time . . . his word and credit was current and would pass in the country with and amongst his neighbours . . . now they make it very scrupulous to take (his) word or promise, yea scarcely his bond for a matter of five pounds': so that he is 'prejudiced and damnified exceedingly not only in his reputation and credit but also in his private estate;' his creditors calling on him 'for their money faster than (he) can provide . . . threatening (him) with arrests and suits, so as (he) dare not stay at home in his own house or in the country, but is forced to fly and obscure himself from his own house, wife, and family, to his exceeding great loss ..."[9]

There are remarkable resonances in this passage: a wool dealer of Warwick, ruining his former partner, John Lee, glover; and Humphrie Grigg of Beaudesert, Warwickshire, daring not to stay at home, for fear of arrest of debt – it all has a highly familiar ring. And there is some evidence that John Shakespeare's reputation had been damaged in the way that Everitt has outlined; not only was he pursued for debt, but in his 1597 submission in the Lambert dispute he stated that "John Lamberte ys of greate wealthe and abilitie, and well frended and alied amongest gentlemen and freeholders of the countrey in the saide countie of

Warwicke, where he dwelleth, and your said oratours are of small wealthe and verey fewe frendes and alyance in the saide countie."[10] This of course might have been exaggeration to elicit the sympathy of the court, but it is compatible with John Shakespeare having lost "credit-worthiness". Everitt also quotes evidence about the rapidity of the rise and fall of traders, which echoes the passage quoted above on Tarquin. Robert Reyce of Suffolk described the kind of trader who "in short time climbeth to much credit and wealth" and "such is the world, which is nothing but a shop of all change, that too often it falleth out for these riches thus hastily gotten, which can abide no enduring continuance, (that) they receive in exchange first decay, which when willingness in suretyship hath laid open too manifestly, then poverty too, too quickly remedyless seizes them."[11]

However, there is no direct evidence that John Shakespeare suddenly lost his credit-worthiness, although there was a very rapid deterioration in his economic position. In about 1576 he applied for a coat of arms and in order to achieve this, the applicant had to "live without manuell labour, and therefore to . . . beare the port, charge and countenance of a gentleman." We are describing a shift from the protestant ethic of the earlier period, when John Shakespeare was building his family fortunes, to this gentlemanly way of life. John Wesley understood this process better than most: "I fear, wherever riches have increased, the essence of religion has decreased in the same proportion. Therefore I do not see how it is possible, in the nature of things, for any revival of true religion to continue long. For religion must necessarily produce both industry and frugality, and these cannot produce riches. But as riches increase, so will pride, anger, and love of the world in all its branches."[12]

Protestantism has always engendered its own particular brand of vulnerability: stripped of the protective rituals, beliefs and practices of traditional Roman Catholicism, Protestants were thrown back on their own psychological resources. Where it was impossible to alleviate a sense of guilt through institutionalised procedures such as the confessional, psychological vulnerabilities were likely to acquire the status of "tragic flaws". That this should take the form of alcoholism in John Shakespeare's case, was partly due to his work as an individual trader; Everitt has described the hazards of working in this way: "When so much bargaining was undertaken in alehouses, inns, and farm-kitchens all manner of abuses might occur. The case of one Richard Snellinge of

London may be taken as typical. Employed by a poulterer of Gracechurch Street 'in journeying and riding to country markets to buy and provide poultry wares,' Snellinge was despatched by his master with two horses 'worth twenty nobles apiece' to Potton in Bedfordshire. Meeting there in 'riotous manner with two country chapmen' from whom he apparently brought poultry, he went to the Sign of the George in Potton and there continued drinking until they were all drunk . . . slept in the stable of the said inn until seven o'clock at night."[13] The element of riot in Richard Snellinge's behaviour is reminiscent of Falstaff and his companions, but we do not have to interpret this too literally to see that John Shakespeare's work as an individual trader, exposed him constantly to alcoholic drink and its effects.

Additionally, there were hazards in living and working in Stratford, particularly for members of the corporation. We saw earlier that Stratford's chief manufacturing activity was the production of malt; this was reflected in the number of its alehouses, taverns and inns. On the 29th April, 1552 there were listed no less than forty-five tipplers (running alehouses), four innkeepers, and two vintners[14] – representing about one tavern or inn to every thirty people (men, women and children) living in Stratford. From council records, there appears to have been no diminution in the numbers of alehouses and inns during the latter half of the sixteenth century – and this was at a time when home brewing was almost universal. The effect on local life was sufficiently disturbing for the Stratford Corporation on the 8th December, 1592 to totally ban all innholders, alehouse keepers and tipplers from serving "any pore Artificer, day laborer, mens servantes or prentises . . . by day or by night (excepte in the tyme of Christmas) upon payne of Imprisonment by the space of thre dayes & thre nightes of them that be the householders & never to sell Any more Ale or Bere wthin this Boroughe."[15] Six years later things had deteriorated to a point whereby the corporation passed a formal motion deploring the effect of drink on the life of the town: "On 27 September [1598] . . . a strong resolution was passed with respect to the 'great disorder' in the borough caused by the Tipplers (otherwise alehouse keepers), 'through their unreasonable strong drink, to the increase of quarrelling and other misdemeanours in their houses, and the further and greater impoverishment of many poor men haunting the said houses, when their wives and children are in extremity of begging ...' "[16]

But the effects of drink were not confined to the poor; the corporation banned the latter from drinking in ale-houses, but they themselves continued to lavishly entertain visiting magistrates, officials, preachers and players with wine and sack – and of course, while John Shakespeare was a member of the council, he would have participated in these entertainments. The corporation used two inns for this purpose: the Bear and the Swan – both located at the end of Henley Street. And we can most aptly conclude this chapter, by quoting from Halliwell-Phillips's description of the Bear based on an inventory taken in about 1603: "The Bear near the foot of the bridge possessed its large hall, its nominated rooms such as the Lion and Talbot chambers, an enormous quantity of house linen, a whole pipe of claret, two butts of sack, and, among its plate, 'one goblet of silver, parcel gilt' "[17] – reminiscent of Mistress Quickly's admonishment of Falstaff in *2,Henry IV:* "Thou didst sweare to mee upon a parcell of gilt Goblet, sitting in my Dolphin-chamber."

CHAPTER 7: THE DEATH OF JOHN SHAKESPEARE AND THE WRITING OF HAMLET

Hamlet was the key play for revealing the secret behind the enigma of Shakespeare's father's life. Why then was this secret revealed there and not in one of the earlier autobiographical plays? If as Freud suggested, *Hamlet* was written in reaction to John Shakespeare's death, questions of significance and meaning would have been part of that response. The dating of *Hamlet* in relation to Shakespeare's father's death is also important because it could tell us a great deal about the psychological context of the play, as well as possibly explaining the shift in tone and content of Shakespeare's later work – the beginning of the "dark period", which ushered in the great tragedies of the 1600s.

But what is the evidence that *Hamlet* was written after September 1601, when John Shakespeare died? The dating of *Hamlet* is a highly contentious issue, much discussed by Shakespeare scholars. The only certain date is that on which it was first registered, 26th July 1602, when it was listed as "A booke called the Revenge of Hamlett Prince Denmarke as yt was latlie Acted by the Lord Chamberlayne his servantes."[1] One of the most important pieces of evidence for dating *Hamlet* is Gabriel Harvey's note in the 1598 Speght edition of Chaucer, which mentioned Shakespeare's "tragedie of Hamlet, Prince of Denmarke". Jenkins has succinctly summarized the evidence as follows:

> "When exactly, after his purchase of the book in 1598, Harvey wrote this note can only be inferred from other allusions in it; and these are strangely conflicting. The inclusion among our 'florishing metricians' of Spenser, who died on 16 January 1599, is apparently not indicative since the same list oddly includes Watson, who died in 1592; but a statement of what 'the Earle of Essex commendes' and what 'the Lord Mountioy makes the like account

of' points to a time not only before Mountjoy was made Earl of Devonshire in July 1603 but before Essex met his death on 25 February 1601."[2]

Jenkins concludes that the balance of evidence is for a date before 25 February 1601, but notes with some perplexity that Harvey also made reference to "Owens new Epigrams", and these were not published until 1606.[3] A number of scholars have pointed out that the reference to the Earl of Essex in the present is not conclusive: it is possible to quote a dead man's critical opinions in the present tense, a point supported by Harvey's description of the long-dead Watson as a 'florishing metrician'. Even the reference to Lord Mountjoy is not conclusive, for as Kirschbaum argued, Elizabethans were not always careful about the use of titles.[4] Given the degree of conflict of evidence, and the confusion about language and chronology, no firm conclusion about the dating of *Hamlet* can be reached from Harvey's note.

The other major evidence for dating the play is the famous "little eyases" passage, which appeared in the Folio edition. The following is a dialogue between Hamlet and Rosencrantz & Guildenstern about the players who have just arrived at the Danish court:

"*Hamlet* . . . what Players are they?
Rosencrantz Euen those you were wont to take delight in the Tragedians of the City.
Hamlet How chances it they trauaile? their residence both in reputation and profit, was better both wayes.
Rosencrantz I thinke their Inhibition comes by the meanes of the late Innouation.
Hamlet Doe they hold the same estimation they did when I was in the City? Are they so follow'd?
Rosencrantz No indeed, they are not.
Hamlet How comes it? doe they grow rusty?
Rosencrantz Nay, their indeauour keepes in the wonted pace; but there is Sir an ayrie of Children, little Yases, that crye out on the top of the question; and are most tyrannically clapp't for't: these are now the fashion, and so be-ratled the common Stages (so they call them) that many wearing Rapiers, are affraide of Goose-quils, and dare scarce come thither.
Hamlet What are they Children? Who maintains 'em? How are they escoted? Will they pursue the Quality no longer than they can sing? Will they not say afterwards if they should grow themselues to common Players (as it is like most if their meanes are no better) their Writers do them wrong, to make them exclaim against their own Succession.
Rosencrantz Faith there ha's bene much to do on both sides: and the Nation holds it no sinne, to tarre them to Controuersie. There was for a while, no money bid for argument, vnless the Poet and the Player went to Cuffes in the Question.

Hamlet Is't possible?
Guildenstern Oh, there ha's beene much throwing about of Braines.
Hamlet Do the Boyes carry it away?
Rosencrantz I that they do my Lord, *Hercules* & his load too."[5]

It is generally recognized that this is a reference to the "war of the theatres", reflecting a dispute mainly between Jonson on the one hand, and Marston and Dekker on the other, which involved a secondary conflict between the private children's theatres and the public playhouses. The dispute appears to have started with Marston's play *Histriomastix*, written in 1599, possibly for the Children of Paul's.[6] Marston portrayed Jonson in the play, and the latter in turn parodied some of Marston's language in his *Every Man Out Of His Humour*, produced at the end of 1599 or the beginning of 1600. Marston's response was *Jack Drum's Entertainment*, acted by the Children of Paul's in about August 1600; in turn, Jonson replied with *Cynthia's Revels*, which was staged in about December 1600 by the Children of the Revels in their newly opened Blackfriars theatre. Marston probably rejoined with *What You Will* in the early spring of 1601, again acted by the Children of Paul's. Jonson's final response was *The Poetaster* – staged by the Children of the Revels – and as this is the key play for understanding the "little eyases" passage in *Hamlet*, it requires careful consideration.

According to the title page of the 1640 Folio edition of *Poetaster*, the play was "First Acted in the yeare 1601. By the then Children of Queene ELIZABETHS CHAPPELL." In the induction to the play, Jonson (who was a notoriously slow writer) tells us that it was written in anticipation of an attack on him in a play yet to be published: "these fifteene weekes/ (So long as since the plot was but an *embrion*)/ Haue I, with burning lights, mixt vigilant thoughts,/ In expectation of this hated play."[7] Although ostensibly set in Rome, virtually the whole of Act 3, Scene iv is devoted to a satirical attack on the writers and players of the public playhouses, which therefore broadens what was a personal dispute between Marston and Jonson, into a "war of the theatres". Jonson appears to have had the Chamberlain's Men particularly in mind (this may have been partly because of the lack of success of his *Every Man Out Of His Humour* with that company), and contrives the following dialogue between Tucca and Histrio, the latter intended probably as a satire on one of the Chamberlain's players:

"TUCCA . . . I would faine come with my cockatrice one day, and see a play; If I knew when there were a good bawdie one: but they say, you ha'

nothing but *humours*, *reuells*, and *satyres*, that girde, and fart at the time, you slaue.
HISTRIO No, I assure you, Captaine, not wee. They are on the other side of *Tyber:* we haue as much ribaldrie in our plaies, as can bee, as you would wish, Captaine: All the sinners, i' the suburbs, come, and applaud our action, daily.
TUCCA I heare, you'll bring me o' the stage there; you'll play me, they say: I shall be presented by a sort of copper-lac't scoundrels of you: life of PLVTO, and you stage me, stinkard; your mansions shall sweat for't, your tabernacles, varlets, your *Globes*, and your *Triumphs*.
HISTRIO Not we, by PHOEBVS, Captaine: doe not doe vs imputation without desert.
TUCCA I wu' not, my good two-penny rascall: reach mee thy neufe. Do'st heare? What wilt thou giue mee a weeke, for my brace of beagles, here, my little point-trussers? you shall ha' them act among yee."[8]

Jonson here is satirically contrasting his own work being performed at the Blackfriars north of the Thames, with the Chamberlain's plays performed at the Globe south of the river, set amongst the "stews" and other places of "disreputable" activity. His reference to "your Globes" indicates that it was the Chamberlain's men that he had in mind, and Tucca's threat that his "little point-trussers" will "act among yee", appears to be a clear reference to the commercial success of the Children of the Revel's company. Jonson probably included Shakespeare in this satire through the figure of Pantolabus, although this mainly showed Shakespeare in a favourable light. The tone of Jonson's satire at times bordered on the offensive – for example, he refers at one point to the players as "punkes decai'd i' their practice"[9] – and there is no doubt that this whole conflict seriously damaged the Chamberlain's Men. Towards the end of Act 4, Scene iv, Jonson puts the following words into the mouths of Tucca and Histrio, concerning Demetrius, a satire on Dekker:

"HISTRIO . . . hee is . . . one DEMETRIVS, a dresser of plaies about the towne, here; we haue hir'd him to abuse HORACE, and bring him in, in a play, with all his gallants ...
TUCCA And: why so, stinkard?
HISTRIO O, it will get vs a huge deale of money (Captaine) and wee haue need on't; for this winter ha's made vs all poorer, then so many staru'd snakes: No bodie comes at vs; not a gentleman, nor a –"[10]

Horace is a reference to Jonson himself, and if this passage is to be believed, Jonson's satirical work for the Children of the Revels had seriously undermined the fortunes of Shakespeare's company. What had previously been a dispute between individual playwrights, had become a serious commercial battle between the private children's companies and the public theatres. Jonson justified his attack on the latter in a special "apologeticall Dialogue: which was only once spoken upon the stage":

> "... three yeeres,/ They did prouoke me with their petulant stiles/ On euery stage: And I at last, vnwilling,/ But weary, I confesse, of so much trouble,/ Thought I would try, if shame could winne vpon 'hem . . . Now, for the Players, it is true, I tax'd 'hem,/ And yet, but some; and those so sparingly . . . If it gaue 'hem meat,/ Or got 'hem clothes. 'Tis well. That was their end."[11]

Although apologetical in tone, Jonson had successfully predicted (through the speech of Histrio) that the Chamberlain's men were going to stage a play attacking him, and that they were going to do this partly to attract back the audience lost to the children's theatres. If we are to believe the "apologeticall Dialogue" this was successful, for "it gaue 'hem meat" and "got 'hem clothes". This presumably was achieved through Dekker's play *Satiromastix*, which was performed in 1601 by the Chamberlain's Men and by the Paul's Children.[12] The play is widely recognized as a reply to Jonson *Poetaster*, as there are many references to the latter which are counters to Jonson's satire.

Shakespeare almost certainly had Jonson's *Poetaster* in mind when writing the "little eyases" passage: "they berattle the common stages" and "their writers do them wrong to make them exclaim against their own succession", i.e. against the adult players of the public theatre. Jonson's play was the major vehicle for this attack on the players, all the more galling because of coming out of the mouths of the "little point- trussers". But Shakespeare also had in mind Dekker's counter- attack : "there has been much to do on both sides." This refers not just to the dispute between Jonson and Marston – both writing for children's theatres – but between Jonson and Dekker, concentrating on Jonson's satire of the public players. The Chamberlain's Men revived their fortunes through the attack on Jonson in *Satiromastix*, evidenced by both Jonson and Shakespeare.

Poetaster was written and first performed in 1601, probably in the Spring of that year ("this winter ha's made vs all poorer, than so many staru'd snakes.") *Satiromastix* followed in response, and presumably took Dekker at least some weeks, if not months, to write; Fredson Bowers, the modern editor of Dekker's works, believes that *Satiromastix* was not completed until after 14 August, on the grounds that it made reference to "*the Whipping a'th Satyre*", a verse satire which was not entered into the Stationer's Register until that date.[13] Shakespeare referred to the "war of the theatres" in the past tense – "There was for a while no money bid for argument unless the poet and the player went to cuffs in the question" – and this almost certainly includes the Chamberlain's Men's attack on Jonson in Dekker's *Satiromastix*. Given the evidence on the date of writing of the latter, it is likely that *Hamlet* was written some while after August 1601.

There is some evidence that the play was written before the Christmas holiday period of 1601. The students of St John's College, Cambridge put on a play known as *The Return from Parnassus*, Part 2, for the Christmas holiday, and in that play, there is a scene where two graduates apply for jobs as writers with the Chamberlain's Men; one of their managers, Kempe, expresses his scepticism as follows: "Few of the vniuersity men pen plaies well, they smell too much of that writer *Ouid*, and that writer *Metamorphoses*, and talke too much of *Prosperina & Jupiter*. Why heres our fellow *Shakespeare* puts them all downe, I and *Ben Jonson* too. O that *Ben Jonson* is a pestilent fellow, he brought vp *Horace* giuing the Poets a pill, but our fellow *Shakespeare* hath giuen him a purge that made him betray his credit."[14]

Horace giving the poets a pill, refers to *Poetaster*, where Horace (Jonson) gives pills to Crispinus (Marston) to make him vomit, but the reference to Shakespeare giving Jonson a purge, has somewhat puzzled Shakespeare scholars. However, on the present reading of the "war of the theatres", the purge referred to is the "little eyases" passage of *Hamlet;* Shakespeare has Hamlet say of the Children's Companies: "Will they not say afterwards if they should grow themselues to common Players (as it is like most if their meanes are no better) their Writers do them wrong, to make them exclaim against their owne Succession?" Here we have a weighty and justified moral attack on Jonson, the purge referred to in the *Parnassus* play. Jonson in his "apologeticall Dialogue" printed in the Quarto of *Poetaster*, registered on the 21st December 1601, refers to his critics but singles out one of them for special comment: "Onely amongst them, I am sorry for/ Some better natures, by the rest so drawne,/ To rune in that vile line" – presumably a reference to Shakespeare and his criticism of Jonson. Thus on this evidence, *Hamlet* must have been written before the end of December, 1601.

One reason why scholars have resisted a date for *Hamlet* in late 1601, is the reference to the "late innovation", which some have interpreted as relating to the abortive Essex rebellion of February 1601. Essex's supporters paid Shakespeare's company, the Lord Chamberlain's Men, for a special performance of *Richard 2* (in which King Richard is deposed and killed), in order to encourage support for the rebellion. As a result, Augustine Phillips was required to explain the Chamberlain's Men's role in the affair[15], and some have suggested that this led to the suppression of the company and its performance of plays in London. But no action was taken against the company, and on the 24th February – the day before Essex's execution – they played before the Queen at Whitehall; it is therefore difficult to give any credence to the argument that the rebellion was the innovation that Shakespeare referred to. That the innovation was a reference to the child actors, is strongly supported by the first Quarto of *Hamlet;* in that edition, the lengthy "little eyases" passage quoted above is severely truncated, and the reason for the players travelling is explicitly given as follows: "noueltie carries it away,/ For the principall publike audience that/ Camc to them, are turned to priuate playes,/ And to the humour of children."[16]

The balance of all the evidence suggests that *Hamlet* was written in late 1601, and probably after John Shakespeare's death in September, and before the Christmas holiday of that year. *Hamlet* is the beginning of an entirely new phase in Shakespeare's work, and represents a radical departure from previous writing. It was the beginning of the period in which Shakespeare wrote most of his great tragedies; on the present argument, it was John Shakespeare's death which was responsible for this radical shift in tone and content. The intensity of Shakespeare's reaction to his father's death is indicated in *Hamlet:* "Remember thee?/ I, thou poore Ghost, while memory holds a seate/ In this distracted Globe: Remember thee?/ Yea, from the Table of my Memory/ Ile wipe away all triuial fond Records,/ All sawes of Bookes, all formes, all pressures past,/ That youth and obseruation coppied there;/ And thy Commandment all alone shall liue/ Within the Booke and Volume of my Braine,/ Vnmixt with baser matter."[17] What clearer manifesto for the ensuing "dark period" could we find? The depth of Hamlet's grief is indicated by both the Queen his mother and Claudius, his uncle King:

> "*Queen* . . . Do not for euer with thy veyled lids/ Seeke for thy Noble Father in thc dust;/ Thou know'st 'tis common, all that liues must dye,/ Passing through Nature, to Eternity …
> *King* 'Tis sweet and commendable in your Nature *Hamlet,*/ To giue these mourning duties to your Father:/ But you must know, your Father lost a Father,/ That father lost his, and the Suruiuer bound/ In filiall Obligation,

> for some terme/ To do obsequious Sorrow. But to perseuer/ In obstinate Condolement, is a course/ Of impious stubbornnesse. 'Tis vnmanly greefe . . . a fault to Nature . . . whose common Theame/ Is death of Fathers, and who still hath cried,/ From the first Coarse, till he that dyed to day,/ This must be so."[18]

That this is not exaggeration used by the King and Queen to undermine Hamlet, is confirmed by Hamlet's own admission to Guilderstern: "... I have of late, but wherefore I know not, lost all my mirth, forgone all custome of exercise; and indeed, it goes so heauily with my disposition, that this goodly frame the Earth, seemes to me a sterill Promontory ..."[19] Grief at the death of a father is a general theme of the play: Hamlet, Ophelia and Laertes all lament the death of their fathers. Orphelia is said to have gone mad as a result of her father's death – "it springs/ All from her father's death" – and perhaps the following song is an appropriate lament for the death of John Shakespeare:

> "They bore him bare fac'd on the Bier,/ Hey non nony, nony, hey nony:/ And on his graue raines many a teare . . . And will he not come againe,/ And will he not come againe:/ No, no, he is dead, go to thy Death-bed,/ He neuer wil come againe./ His Beard as white as Snow,/ All Flaxen was his Pole:/ He is gone, he is gone, and we cast away mone: Gramercy on his Soule."[20]

We can make no better conclusion to the main argument of this section of the book than quote from *Hamlet*, as an epitaph on John Shakespeare: "Alas poore *Yoricke*, I knew him *Horatio*, a fellow of infinite jest, of most excellent fancie, hee hath bore me on his backe a thousand times, and now how abhorred in my imagination it is: my gorge rises at it. Heere hung those lyppes that I have kist I know not howe oft, where be your gibes now? your gamboles? your songs, your flashes of merriment ..."[21]

SECTION II

"Stratford Bridge" (From Samuel Ireland, Picturesque Views on the Warwickshire Avon *[1795])*

Barton-On-The-Heath, Warwickshire

"The House in which Shakespeare was Born" (From William Smith, A New and Compendious History of the County of Warwick *[1830])*

"View of Charlecote Deer Park" (From William Smith, A New and Compendious History of the County of Warwick *[1830])*

"The Deer Barn" (Drawn by W. Jackson in 1798).

"View of Weston Hall" (*From William Smith,* A New and Compendious History of the County of Warwick *[1830]*)

The Bust of William Shakespeare, in Stratford Parish Church

CHAPTER 8: THE DEER POACHING TRADITION

As we have seen, one of the most autobiographical of the plays is *The Merry Wives Of Windsor*, and there are a number of passages which have been generally recognized as applying to Shakespeare himself. The comical cross-examination of Mistress Page's son William on his Latin grammar by Parson Hugh Evans, has suggested to most commentators Shakespeare's own experience with the Stratford schoolmaster Thomas Jenkins – and Mistress Page's comment to Sir Hugh that "my husband saies my sonne [William] profits nothing in the world at his Booke", has echoes of the tradition that Shakepeare was prematurely withdrawn from school because of his father's economic difficulties.[1] Likewise the character of Gentle Master Fenton is consistent with what we know of Shakespeare as a young man; as the host in the play describes him: "He capers, he dances, he has eies of youth: he writes verses, hee speakes holiday, he smels April and May." At the end of the play, Fenton runs away with Ann Page and marries her very much against her parents' wishes – reminiscent of Shakespeare's hurried marriage to Anne Hathaway. But most important of all, is the wildness of Fenton's youth: "The Gentleman is of no hauing, he kept companie with the wilde Prince, and *Pointz:* he is of too high a Region, he knows too much" – an accusation which is admitted by Fenton himself, confessing to his "Riots past, my wilde Societies."

This brings us to the most important of all the autobiographical themes in *The Merry Wives Of Windsor:* the poaching of deer from Justice Shallow, reputedly based on the local magistrate, Sir Thomas Lucy. The two main accounts of this story are those told by Richard Davies and Nicholas Rowe. Davies wrote at the end of the seventeenth century: [Shakespeare was] "much given to all unluckinesse in stealing venison & rabbits particularly from Sr [Thomas] Lucy who had him oft whipt &

sometimes imprisoned & at last made him fly his native country to his great advancement. But his reveng was so great that he [Lucy] is his Justice Clodplate [Shallow] and calls him a great man & yt in allusion to his name bore three lowses rampant for his Arms."[2] Rowe wrote a somewhat fuller version of the story in his biography of Shakespeare, published in 1709:

> "He [Shakespeare] had, by misfortune common enough to young fellows, fallen into ill company; and amongst them, some that made a frequent practice of Deer-stealing, engag'd him with more than once in robbing a park that belong'd to Sir Thomas Lucy of Cherlecot, near Stratford. For this he was prosecuted by that Gentleman, as he thought, somewhat too severely; and in order to revenge that ill usage, he made a ballad upon him. And tho' this, probably the first essay of his poetry, be lost, yet it is said to have been so very bitter, that it redoubled the prosecution against him to that degree, that he was oblig'd to leave his business and family in Warwickshire, for some time, and shelter himself in London."[3]

The fullest account of this ballad is that published by Edward Capell; Capell described how this version came into his hands:

> "One stanza of it, which has the appearance of genuine, was put into the editor's hands many years ago by an ingenious gentleman (grandson of its preserver) with this account of the way it descended to him. – Mr Thomas Jones, who dwelt at Tarbick [Tardebigge] a village in Worcestershire a few miles from Stratford-on-Avon, and dy'd in the year 1703 aged upwards of ninety, remember'd to have heard from several old people at Stratford the story of Shakespeare's robbing Sir Thomas Lucy's park; and their account of it agreed with Mr Rowe's, with this addition – that the ballad written against Sir Thomas by Shakespeare was stuck upon his park gate, which exasperated the knight to apply to a lawyer at Warwick to proceed against him: Mr Jones had put down in writing the first stanza of this ballad, which was all that he remember'd of it, and Mr Thomas Wilkes (my grandfather) transmitted it to my father by memory, who also took it in writing, and his copy is this: 'A parliamente member a justice of peace,/ At Home a poore Scarecrow at London an asse./ If Lowsie is Lucy as some Volke miscalle it/ then Lucy is Lowsie whatever befalle it/ He thinkes himself greate/ Yet an asse is his state/ we allowe by his eares but with asses to mate/ If Lucy is Lowsie as some Volke miscalle it/ Sing (O) Lowsie Lucy whatever befalle it'."[4]

Two of these three accounts of the poaching incident either state or imply that it took place at Sir Thomas Lucy's park at Charlecote. Towards the end of the eighteenth century, a new tradition emerged which relocated the incident to a neighbouring deer park at Fulbrook. The first person to put this tradition into print was John Jordan, a self-educated local wheelwright, who collected a number of stories about Shakespeare. Jordan's version of the incident, written in 1790, is as follows:

> "[Sir Thomas Lucy] had at the time also another park at a place called Fullbroke, two miles distant from the other; and there tradition reports it was that Shakespeare and his companions made a practise of following their favourite diversion; which they did so often, that the knight's resentment was raised, and he commenced a prosecution against them, but desisted upon their making an abject submission; but which so hurt the high spirit of our poet that he could not repress his idignation. A satirical song went abroad, which inflamed Sir Thomas to the utmost pitch, and he renewed the prosecution with redoubled vigour. His power was too great for poor Shakespeare to contend with, and he now saw, perhaps with horror, that his youthful levity obliged him to quit his father, his fond wife, his prattling babes, and his native place."[5]

In 1788, the Rev. S. Cooper, of Loxley, had written to Jordan, mentioning a farm "at Ingon containing now about two hundred acres of land adjoining to the old park, now deparked, from which it is said William Shakespeare stole Mr Lucy's deer."[6] This may be a reference to Fulbrook, but will be discussed when an evaluation is made of the historical accuracy of the poaching tradition. A further claim that the poaching took place at Fulbrook was made by Samuel Ireland in 1795:

> "It was in this [Fulbrook] park our bard is said to have been, in a youthful frolic, engaged in stealing deer, and thereby to have drawn upon himself a prosecution from the then owner, Sir Thomas Lucy . . . Within this park is now standing, on a spot called Daisy Hill, a farm house, which was antiently the keeper's lodge. To this lodge it is reported our Shakespeare was conveyed, and there confined at the time of the charge, which is supposed to have been brought against him."[7]

Sir Walter Scott is thought to have referred to Fulbrook when he made a note in his diary in 1828 at the time of a visit to Charlecote:

> "April 8 . . . Charlecote is in high preservation, and inhabited by Mr Lucy, descendant of the worshipful Sir Thomas . . . He told me the park from which Shakespeare stole the buck was not that which surrounds Charlecote, but belonged to a mansion at some distance, where Sir Thomas resided at the time of the trespass. The tradition went that they hid the buck in a barn, part of which was standing a few years ago, but now totally decayed. This park no longer belongs to the Lucys."[8]

According to Lady Alice Fairfax-Lucy, George Lucy who had told Scott the above, "had busied himself with collecting a vast mass of notes on Lucy genealogy."[9] A separate reference to the deer barn was given by W.Jackson, who had made a drawing of it in 1798; under his engraving –

which was headed "GROVE FIELD, WARWICKSHIRE - THE DEER BARN" – he wrote:

> "This barn was originally appropriate to the use of foddering the deer belonging to the park which formerly surrounded this place of antiquity. Here it was that the immortal Shakespeare secreted himself after he had stolen the deer. Charlecote is the name of the family seat of the Lucys, and there belongs to it a park well stocked with deer; but there remains a doubt in my mind whether it ever belonged to the park where this barn stands, as the river Avon runs close by the extremities of the present park, and that which originally [was a park] is now converted into farms."[10]

Jackson was confused about the location of the deer barn in relation to the park from which the deer were poached, but we will see later that this confusion was understandable given the number of parks that the Lucy family were linked with in the sixteenth century. According to the local historian of Stratford-on-Avon, R. B. Wheeler, writing at the beginning of the nineteenth century, "the uniformly believed opinion and tradition [in the locality] is that it [the poaching incident] happened at Charlecote."[11] This statement will be evaluated in discussion of a review of the historical and documentary evidence. There were other references to the deer-poaching tradition in the eighteenth and nineteenth centuries, but they add little to the accounts quoted above, with the exception of one unusual twist to the story quoted by Sir Richard Phillips in 1818: "At Stratford, the family maintain that Shakespeare stole Sir Thomas Lucy's buck, to celebrate his wedding day, and for that purpose only ..."[12]

We therefore see that there was a large body of local and oral evidence in favour of the poaching tradition, and given that some of the evidence is from independent sources, we would normally expect it to be widely accepted. Some scholars have rejected the tradition partly on the basis of the argument that it is simply an embellishment of Falstaff's raiding of Justice Shallow's park in *The Merry Wives Of Windsor*. But there are a number of flaws in this line of argument: there was a cony warren at Charlecote and although there is no mention of rabbit poaching in *The Merry Wives Of Windsor*, Davies mentions Shakespeare poaching rabbits as well as deer. Also Davies was unfamiliar with the details of *The Merry Wives Of Windsor* for he calls Shallow "Justice Clodplate"; his account of the story remained in manuscript form and was not known to Rowe when he wrote his version. Rowe derived his account from local tradition (this was collected by the Shakespearian actor, Betterton, who according to Rowe made a special journey into Warwickshire some time during the second half of the seventeenth century to collect information on Shakespeare.) Where Rowe's information can be checked against independent documentary evidence it has turned out to be accurate – the major example of this being his statement that John Shakespeare was a dealer in wool.

The multiplicity of separate sources for the poaching story would in itself suggest that it was genuine. Sir Thomas Lucy was a Member of Parliament and in March 1585 had charge of a bill "for the preservation for grain and game" – which is certainly consistent with the traditional accounts of his reaction to the poaching of his deer. The association between Justice Shallow and Lucy is suggested by their similar coat of arms; Shallow had "a dozen white Luces", whereas Sir Thomas Lucy had three white luces (see Plate 1) – although on at least one occasion his coat is known to have been "quartered" [reminiscent of Slender's remark on Shallow's coat: "I may quarter (Coz)."], producing a dozen white luces.[13] Most scholars have been prepared to accept that the traditional testimony for the poaching story is strong, but the major difficulty in its acceptance has been the absence of any firm evidence for a deer park at Charlecote or Fulbrook at the relevant period. However, the lack of such evidence is largely due to the failure of Shakespeare scholars to take the poaching tradition seriously, and this evidence will now be considered in some detail.

WINDOW AT CHARLECOTE WITH LUCY ARMS

Plate 1: The Arms Of Sir Thomas Lucy (From Edgar I. Fripp, Shakespeare's Haunts New Stratford *[1929])*

CHAPTER 9:
SIR THOMAS LUCY'S DEER PARKS

The formal legal history of licensed deer parks only provides limited information on their actual existence. Jane Croom, the historian of medieval deer parks in Warwickshire, has summarised the position very succinctly for the period 1100-1530:

> "The Patent and Charter Rolls record royal licences to create parks, but only seven [out of a total of seventy-nine] were issued for Warwickshire, so for the majority of parks the actual date of emparking is not known, and we have only the date of the earliest reference . . . However, it seems unlikely that it was always necessary to obtain a royal licence to empark. Only 290 licences are known for the whole of England ..."[1]

The first mention of a park at Charlecote was in 1486, when Rous wrote his account of the enclosure and depopulation of villages in Warwickshire; he stated that almost all of Charlecote was emparked and that the population had fallen from forty-two people in the seventh year of the reign of Edward I to seven people in 1486.[2] In 1510 a Sir Thomas Lucy (Shakespeare's Sir Thomas Lucy's grandfather) owned "20 acres of wood, one park, several fisheries in the water of the Avon . . . in the Manor of Charlecote."[3] In the same year he was granted, as one of the King's sewers, the keepership of Fulbrook Park, and fifteen years aftwerwards in 1525 there is record of his ownership of "unus parcus".[4] Given his ownership of a park in Charlecote in 1510, this almost certainly again refers to Charlecote, and in June of 1525 his steward, Richard Cocks, wrote from Charlecote to Lucy's wife in London, sending her venison, adding that a "buck killed for Master Nethermill had an ill liver" and he "doubted of more".[5] In 1557, Shakespeare's Sir Thomas Lucy acquired the manors of Bishop's Hampton and Hatton, which included what had previously in 1549 been known as Hampton Park.[6] In 1594, legal note was made of the existence of a warren at Charlecote [7], whereas in 1618 Sir Thomas Lucy's grandson obtained a patent to impale on his estates, " the *parcum vocatum* Charlecote Park *in Comitatu Warwicensi*" and "the *parcum vocatum* Sutton Park *in Comitatu Wigorniensi*"[8], the latter being a deer park in Worcestershire that was inherited by Lucy through marriage during the middle of the sixteenth century.

Although useful as backround, the legal history of the status of Sir Thomas Lucy's parks and warrens does not in itself answer the question that we are mainly interested in: the existence of a park/warren at the time of Shakespeare's alleged poaching activities – some time during the middle of the 1580's. The existence of a legal right does not mean that it was necessarily exercised, and conversely Elizabethans invariably ignored the law when it suited their convenience – witness John Shakespeare's moneylending and woolbroking activities. We therefore need to examine the evidence for the existence of a park/warren beyond the legal record in some detail. Our starting point must be the Lucy Household Accounts Book, which covers the period 1573-1587.[9] The first quarterly entry in 1573 (for the second quarter of the year) includes the following listing of names and wages paid:

"Tho. Eden keper at Char. warren -------- x s.
Jo. Morrysse, keper there lykwyse -------- xiii s. iiij d.
Wm Hulett, keper at Hatton -------- x s.
Jo. Rowbery, keper there also --------- vj s. viij d."

There was no keeper mentioned for Sutton, although there was a "balyfe", and by implication, from the sequence of the listing, a "keper of horse" and a "fawlconer" at that place. The next quarter's listing was identical, as was the final quarter except that Richard Lawson replaced John Morrysse as under-keeper at Charlecote and a second "ffawlkoner" was apparently added at Sutton. The same listing continued into the first quarter of 1574, with the addition of an extra falconer, which was also carried over into the second quarter – although by then, at least one of the three – John Gowlde – was working at Charlecote, and possibly one of them was working at Hatton. In the third quarter, both the keepers listed for Hatton disappeared, as did one of the falconers – leaving two keepers (Thomas Eden and Richard Lawson) and one falconer (John Gowlde) at Charlecote, and one falconer and a keeper of horse at Sutton. This pattern of just the two keepers at Charlecote was maintained until the third quarter of 1575, when for the first time a "keper of Sutton parke" was listed.

The pattern of two keepers at Charlecote and one at Sutton was then maintained until 1578, in which year William Hullett, who had been one of the keepers at Hatton, appeared as head keeper at Charlecote. In the following year the two Charlecote keepers disappeared and did not re-appear until three years later during the second quarter of 1582, when Sir Thomas Lucy began to keep his own account book, stating that he had "payd to hidgcox keaper of my conynove ------ £iij xv s." This very large wage – something like seven times the normal wage of an ordinary head keeper – was paid to Hidgcox until the third quarter of 1583, when he suddenly disappeared from the record. He had been the only keeper at Charlecote during this one-and-a-half year period, and probably was responsible for the construction of a completely new warren at Charlecote, given Sir Thomas Lucy's reference to a "conynove".

During this whole period – 1575-1583 – only one keeper was maintained at Sutton, and this appears to have continued right through to the end of the account book in 1587. After Hidgcox left Charlecote in 1583, there were no keepers listed there for the last quarter of that year and the first quarter of the following year. But in the second quarter of 1584, "xj s. viij d." was "payd to robert mathew my keeper" at Charlecote, who was replaced by "wylliam mathew" in the following quarter. In the final quarter of 1584 a second "cony keeper" (Thomas Reynolds) was added to the list for Charlecote, and the pattern of two keepers (they were invariably referred to as "my keeper" and "my other keeper") was maintained right through to the end of the record in 1587.

Although the account book tells us a great deal about what was happening at Charlecote and elsewhere, in some ways it raises more problems than it solves. In particular, there are the very puzzling references to the two keepers at Hatton during the first two years of the account in 1573 and 1574. In 1551, Sir Thomas Lucy's father, William Lucy, had owned the manor of Shrewley in the parish of Hatton, Warwickshire, but this manor had been sold to Clement Throckmorton by 1561.[10] However, Sir Thomas Lucy had acquired the manor of Hatton (also known as Hayton), along with that of Bishop's Hampton, both in the parish of Bishop Hampton (afterwards known as Hampton Lucy), in 1557.[11] There is some confusion over the exact whereabouts of the manor of Hatton, the author of the *Victorian County History of Warwickshire* article on Hatton, maintained that "Lands in 'a field called Grove Field' in the tenure of William Lucy are specifically mentioned in the grant of the manor to Thomas Lucy in 1557."[12] The same author went on to argue that Hampton Woods was probably identical with Hampton Park, which had been owned during the medieval period by the Bishop of Worcester, and therefore this park adjoined Grovefield. He reached this conclusion partly on the basis that a forester had a holding at the Grove in the late twelth century, suggesting that this was the location for Hampton Park.[13]

The reader will perhaps remember the earlier reference to William Jackson's drawing of the deer barn in Grovefield, in which it was alleged that Shakespeare hid. The existence of a deer park at this site – even a few years earlier than the probable date of the poaching incident – would obviously be of very great interest in assessing the poaching tradition. However, it appears that the *V.C.H.* author was incorrect in his conclusions, although it is a matter we must examine in some detail. In 1557 the Crown sold to Thomas Lucy for £989.19s.6d. the "reversion and reversions of the aforesaid manor and manors of Hampton Episcopi and Hatton" which had lately been seized from the Duke of Northumberland on his attainder and conviction for high treason. This grant was to include "all those lands tenements meadows feeding pastures and hereditaments with appurtenances severally lying in the aforesaid Hampton Episcopi in a certain field called Grovefield in the parish of Hampton ... being and in our hands through purchase . . . from Ralph Sadler Knight lately belonging to the advowson . . . to the Rectory and Parish Church of Hampton Episcopi."[14] It would appear from this that Grovefield was not a part of the manor of Hatton, in that it was purchased quite separately.

A listing was made in 1602 of the recently deceased Sir Thomas Lucy's lands, which further clarifies the position; a reference was made to "Grovefield except woods and lands called Hampton Wood", implying that the latter was a part of the former. In the same listing a description of the legal basis of ownership and value of the various lands was given as follows:

> "Manor of Hampton Episcopi from the Queen in Chief value clear per annum £20 & lands called Hayton alias Hatton & pastures and meadows of which they are ignorant [value per annum] £5.2.0. and lands called Grovefield from the Queen as of the manor of Warwick in common socage value clear per annum £5.2.8 and the advowson & parsonage of the Church of Hampron Episcopi and a hereditament called Hampton Wood from the Queen as of Manor of Warwick in common socage value clear per annum £5.15.3."[15]

This list clearly states that neither Grovefield nor Hampton Woods were a part of Hatton Manor, but on the contrary were part of the manor of Warwick. This also destroys the linkage of Hampton Park with Hampton Woods, as the former was a part of the manor of Bishops Hampton, whereas the latter was a part of the manor of Warwick. The location of Hampton Park therefore remains something of a mystery. When it was transferred from the Bishop of Worcester to the Duke of Northumberland in 1549, it was still referred to as Hampton Park, but as a part of "the bishop's woods in Warwickshire called Hampton Parke and Busshe Woods."[16] It is possible that Hampton Park was located in Hatton, as the "descent of the manor of HATTON follows that of the main manor [of Hampton Lucy] throughout,"[17] and although Hampton Park is listed as being a part of the manor of Bishop's Hampton, it may be that there was some confusion over this. However, there is no indication of any deer park in Hatton at any point in its history – it is not mentioned for example in Croom's study of Warwickshire parks – and the likely solution lies elsewhere: in the highly complicated and obscure history of Fulbrook Park.

★ ★ ★

The manor of Hatton was described in a special act of Parliament confirming title of certain of Sir Thomas Lucy's lands in 1585, as "all those closes pastures, meadowes and heredytamentes in the saide parishe of Bushoppes Hampton and commonly called of knowen by the name of or names of Hayton or Hatton Leasowes."[18] Although there is no description of the location of Hatton at this time, we are fortunate in having a very detailed survey and plan of the area for the year 1736.[19] This was prepared by James Fish, a surveyor from Warwick, and his work enables us to study in some detail the question not only the location of Hatton, but its relationship to neighbouring Fulbrook Park.(See Plate 2) Hatton stretched from Ox Close adjoining the river, across to Great Ground, south of Hobbins Ground, on the right-hand side. This latter part of Hatton was known as Blackhills Farm, and directly adjoined the area of Fulbrook designated by Fish as The Old Park. Long Close and Highway Close were a part of The Old Park, and were listed by Fish as "next Black Hills", and so Blackhill Farm in Hatton was directly adjacent to The Old Park in Fulbrook.

Fish locates "Fullbrook Parke" in the centre of the area designated by him as The Old Park – and this is exactly the location of Daisy Hill Farm, the lodge that Shakespeare is alleged to have been taken to after

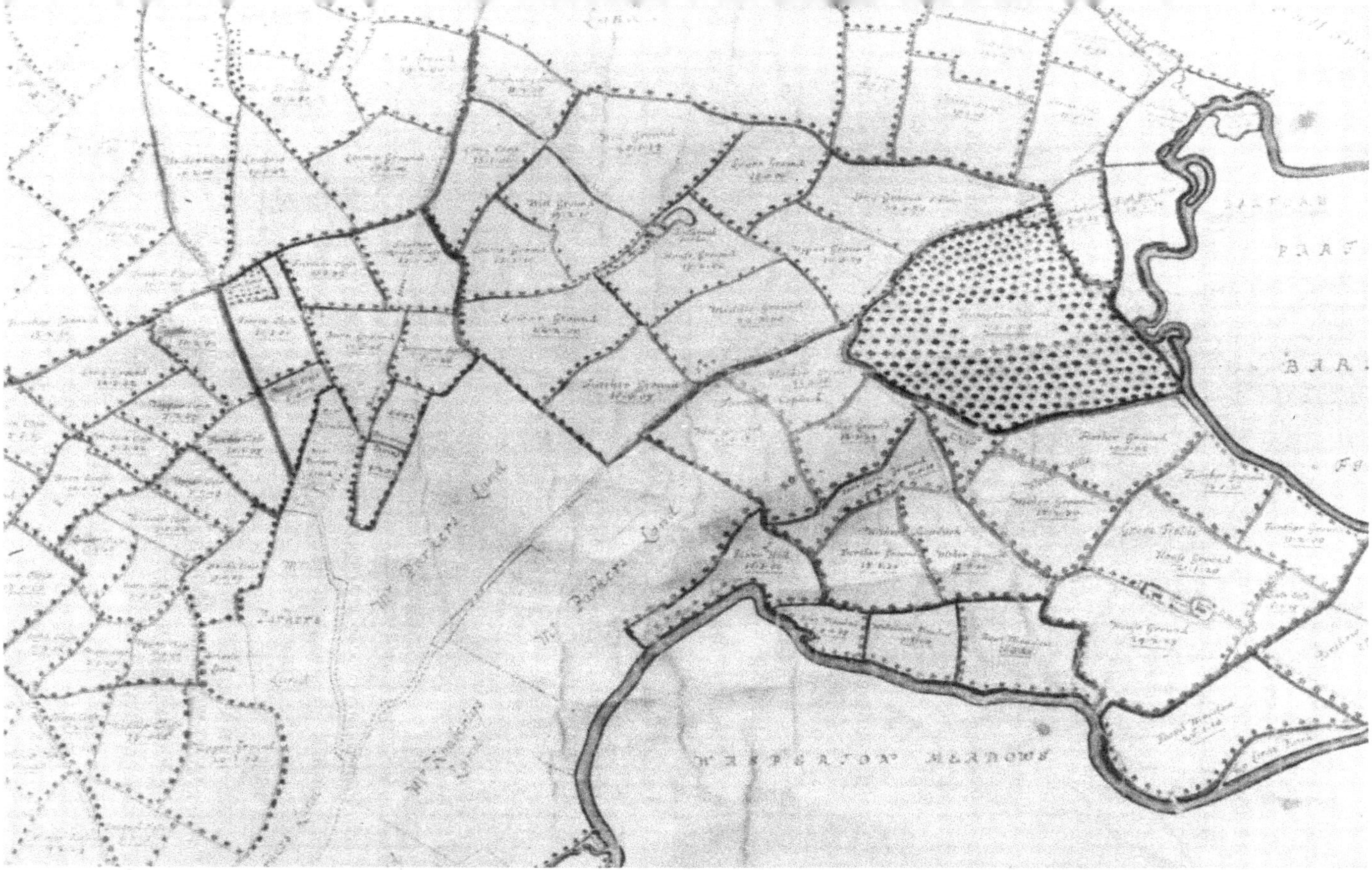

Plate 2: Fulbrook Park and Surrounding Area (From James Fish, The Survey Book of Charlecote etc *[1736] in Warwick C.R.O.)*

capture.(See Plate 2) But why should Sir Thomas Lucy place his keepers in an area adjacent to Fulbrook, and why did he withdraw them in 1574? In order to answer this question, we must now review what is known about the history of Fulbrook Park. The best introduction to the subject is the *The Victorian County History of Warwickshire's* summary:

> "According to Rous, the Warwick antiquary, the once celebrated park of Fulbrook, near Warwick, was inclosed early in the reign of Henry VI by John, Duke of Bedford, brother of Henry V. On the accession of Edward IV the manor and park passed to the crown, and . . . Henry VIII, at the beginning of his reign, granted the custody of the park to Thomas Lucy, to hold during pleasure. Leland, writing towards the end of this reign, mentions 'the fayre parke called Fulbroke', adding that 'the praty castle made of stone and bricks was an eyesore to the Earles that lay in Warwick castle, and was cause of displeasure between each Lord,' until Sir William Compton, as keeper of Fulbrook castle and park, seeing it go to ruin, helped it forward and took much of it to build his house at Compton Wyniates. In the days of James I the park, which had been purchased by Sir Thomas Lucy, was much enlarged."[20]

The author of another article on Fulbrook in the *Victorian County History* adds some additional detail to this account:

> "The boundaries of the . . . park inclosed by John, Duke of Bedford, [in] about 1421 . . . [are] known to have extended from the river up to the Stratford [to Warwick] road and Rous [writing before 1486] complains bitterly that the inclosing of the park converted a formerly safe highway into a notorious haunt of robbers, who lay in wait for their victims behind the newly erected palings."[21]

After the park passed to the crown, its rights of keepership were granted to a number of different favourites of the king; as we have previously seen, Thomas Lucy, one of the king's sewers, was appointed keeper of the park "during pleasure" in the year 1510.[22] Sixteen years later, in 1526, it was granted to William Corpson, one of the Yeoman of the Guard [23]; and in 1534, it was granted to Thomas Ogle, one of the Riders of the King's Horse, as a reversion on Corpson's death.[24] In the late 1530's, Leland gave his account of a visit to Fulbrook as follows: "I roade from Warwicke to Bareford Bridge of 8 fayre arches a 2 miles [from Warwicke]. Here I sawe halfe a mile lower upon Avon on the right ripe by northe a fayr parke caullyd Fulbroke."[25]

So when it was bought by John Dudley, Duke of Northumberland from the crown in 1547[26], it was still "a fayr parke". In 1557 it was said that "the premisses before the late Duke of Northumberland's time were 'A parke replenyshid with deare and by him disparked and all the woods sold and the pale taken awaye.' "[27] On the attainder of the Duke of Northumberland in 1553, Fulbrook was granted to the Catholic Sir Francis Englefield by the new Queen Mary; Englefield was appointed Keeper of Fulbrook Park for life, "with all fees and profits pertaining to that office and profits and revenues of Manor of Fulbrooke."[28] On the 22nd December 1557, Englefield bought Fulbrook, along with lands in Cholsey, Berkshire, for £254.15s.; and he was granted: "... the reversions of the said capital mansion and lands in Cholsey and of the said herbage and pannage of Fulbrooke Park . . . lands called 'Fulbroke Parke' in Fulbroke, co. Warwick, and divers lands (*described*) within or without the bounds of the said park . . . now disparked . . . Yearly value . . . £14.12s.6d. . . . [and for Englefield] To hold [Cholsey and] Fulbroke Park in chief by the service of one- fortieth part of a knight's fee ..."[29]

With the accession of Elizabeth, Englefield's Catholic sympathies brought him into immediate conflict with the crown, and there ensued a series of confused and complicated events which threw title of possession of Fulbrook into great doubt. The *Dictionary of National Biography* gives a summary of events which provides a useful background:

> "Sir Francis Englefield . . . Being a firm adherent of the catholic religion, he fled abroad in 1559, soon after the accession of Elizabeth, and retired to Valladolid. His lands and goods were seized to the queen's use in consequence of his disobedience in not coming home after the queen's revocation, and for consorting with her enemies . . . Subsequently he was attainted and convicted of high treason in parliament on 29 Oct.1585, and all his manors, lands and vast possessions were declared to be forfeited to the crown . . . Englefield had however, by indenture dated in the eighteenth year of the queen's reign (1575-6), settled his manor and estate of Englefield on Francis, his nephew, with power notwithstanding of revoking the grant if he should deliver or tender a gold ring to his nephew. Various disputes and points of law arose as to whether the Englefield estate was forfeited to the queen. After protracted discussions in the law courts the question remained undecided, and accordingly the queen in the ensuing parliament (35th Eliz.) had a special statute passed to confirm the attainder and to establish the forfeiture to herself. After tendering by her agents a ring to Englefield, the nephew, she seized and confiscated the property . . . alienated and transferred to the crown."[30]

In fact, the above is a somewhat simplified account of what happened to Englefield's property. The crown had seized Englefield's lands in Berkshire and Wiltshire in 1563, but had allowed his wife, Catherine, the income from some of this property, as well as allowing Englefield's sister-in-law Margaret (wife to his brother John) £40 a year for maintenance.

Englefield himself had been allowed to keep £300 a year and more, which had been frozen to £300 in 1571 because of his continuing refusal to return to England.[31] (The seizure of lands on the one hand and yet allowance of income on the other, was all part of a long political struggle which took place between Elizabeth and the Catholic opposition.) The position on Fulbrook was described on the 7th October 1573 in a commission, conducted by Sir Thomas Lucy and others, "to enquire concerning the death of Francis Englefield overseas":

> "Inrots say that Francis Englefield was seized as of fee of 1 messuage 20 acres of meadow 350 acres pasture and 100 acres woods called Fulbroke Park in Fulbrook in Warwickshire value £40 per annum . . . by an indenture of 6 May 1 Elizabeth granted the same to Edward Fytton Ralph Egerton Kt John Mayor Esq John Corbet gent and Richard Bosne yeoman to be held for the use of Francis Englefield during the life of John Englefield Esq deceased the brother of Francis and after the death of John for the use of Margaret his wife, sister of Edward Fytton for her life and after her death for the use of Francis Englefield and his heirs . . . Francis had licence to stay overseas for 2 years but stayed after that time and John Engerfield died 3 April 9 Elizabeth . . . and Margaret is alive at Englefield in Berkshire and William Compson is in occupation of the premises at Fulbroke for an unknown term ..."[32]

In fact Sir Francis Englefield did not die until about 1596 (this "mistake" about his death may or may not be significant), and on the face of it, the facts appear fairly straightforward. The crown had allowed Englefield's friends to act as trustees to ensure that the rental income from the property was used for Englefield himself during his brother's lifetime, and then for his sister-in-law on his brother's death. The land was presumably under lease to William Compson for an unknown term, and if this were the case, he would pay the £40 a year rent which would meet Margaret Englefield's annuity. In 1572 the crown began directly collecting the rent from Fulbrook, and this may have represented yet a further hardening of the relationship between the crown and Englefield.[33] We know how the earlier arrangement worked through a complaint that Lady Englefield made about another property of hers that was let under lease; in about 1576, she gave her version of what had happened to the Englefield property at Compton, Berkshire, which had been leased to one Stafford. Lady Englefield complained that although Stafford had obtained a lease on the property for £30 a year, paying the rent to her friends, he had "much absented himself . . . whereby the house ran much to decay" (having his own main residence elsewhere in the county) and "he also let out the arable land and grounds to others, to the spoil thereof."[34] Presumably a similar arrangement operated at Fulbrook, i.e. the estate was let out on lease and then possibly sub-let to a third party; but in its case, the crown was responsible for collecting rent after 1571. All the more surprising then, to find the following entry in the Calendar of Patent Rolls for 27 April 1573: "Licence for Edward Graunt to alienate lands in Fulbroke, co.Warwick, to Thomas Lucy, Knight, John Somervyle and Henry Rogers to the use of Edward and Anne his wife and his heirs and assigns. For 32s. in the Hanaper." This licence is so important that we must quote it in some detail:

> "The Queen to all to whom etc. Greeting . . . Know that we of our special grace and for thirty shillings paid into our hanaper, granted and gave licence . . . to our beloved Edward Grant, gentleman, that he one messuage, twenty acres of land, forty acres of meadow, three hundred acres of pasture and ten acres of woodland, with appurtenances in Fulbrook in our County of Warwick which are held from us in chief so that he can give and grant, alienate, enfeoff or take cognizance of by fine or by recovery in our court of our Justice of the Bench at Westminster or any other way whatsoever at his will, to beloved and faithful Thomas Lucy Knight and our beloved John Somerville, Esquire and Henry Rogers, Gentleman ..."[35]

There was a total of 370 acres included in this licence. It is not known whether it was activated: a search of the Feet of Fines for Warwickshire has not turned up a confirmation of the sale, although when Grant died in 1596, there was no mention of Fulbrook in the post-mortem inquiry – presumptive evidence that the land had been transferred out of his hands. Grant owned an estate at Northbrook in the parish of Fulbrook, but an examination of the relevant estate papers reveals that Northbrook contained only 179 acres, and even if we add extra land owned by Grant at Brierly in Fulbrook, this only gives a total of about 220 acres – 150 acres short of the amount described in the licence.[36] Fulbrook Park was described in an inquisition on the land carried out by Sir Thomas Lucy and others on 19 June 1573, as "1 messuage, 20 acres of meadow, 350 acres of pasture and 1 acre of woodland"[37]: 371 acres of land – nearly identical to the 370 acres described in the licence. There is therefore no doubt that the licence was referring to a transfer of Fulbrook Park to Sir Thomas Lucy and others. However, there are certain features of these transactions which are very puzzling: for example, why was Edward Grant's name not mentioned in the October 1573 inquiry? A part of the solution to this puzzle might lie in the fact that Edward Grant was a member of a prominent Catholic family, and may have been acting in concert with the Englefields to protect their land. He was certainly capable of acting outside of the law: he is the same Edward Grant who sold wool illegally to John Shakespeare two years previously, and his family later became involved in the Somerville conspiracy to kill the Queen. The *Victorian County History* describes Northbrook as follows:

> "At Northbrook . . . [is] the . . . manor house of the Grants, a centre of Catholic disaffection in the reigns of Elizabeth and James I. Edward Grant of Northbrook was described in 1564 as 'an adversary of true religion'. He married Anne Somerville of Edstone and the house was searched in November 1583 after the discovery of his nephew John Somerville's plot against the Queen. His grandson was drawn into the Gunpowder Plot . . . Northbrook was the scene of frequent meetings of the conspirators during 1605."[38]

Edward Grant could have acted in concert with the Englefields to prevent the crown from seizing their land. When Sir Francis Englefield's nephew and heir, Francis Englefield, was examined by Sir John Perrott about his uncle's lands, and "willed to tell the truth, he said the truth is not to be told at all times."[39] The Englefields had tried to save their lands through internal transfer; these evasive devices were sufficiently successful to force the crown to resort to special act of parliament. But although it is credible to believe that Edward Grant acted in concert with the Englefields, it is difficult to see how an ardent Protestant like Sir Thomas Lucy would have done so. However, the partners in the proposed purchase of Fulbrook in the 1573 licence were John Somerville and Henry Rogers – and John Somerville was one of Warwickshire's most prominent Catholics (it was his son John Sommerville who was later executed for plotting against the Queen.[40]) Lucy was clearly friendly with Somerville – he appeared on the commission post-mortem on his lands when he died in 1578[41] – and it is possible that local gentry families acted in concert to protect their lands when threatened by outside forces, like the crown. However, the licence quite clearly referred to Fulbrook being held by Grant from the crown, and therefore there is no direct evidence of any concealment in these arrangements. One alternative explanation of the anomaly of dates, is that there was a mistake in the date of the 1573 licence, and that this was issued after 1574/1575 when the crown stopped collecting rent from Fulbrook. This puzzle can only be settled through future research.

The other party to the proposed purchase of Fulbrook – Henry Rogers – is of great interest in his own right. Rogers was a lawyer and not only was he Sir Thomas Lucy's steward but he was listed in Lucy's account book for the year 1580 as "ffyrst retayner"; he was also town clerk and steward to the Stratford Corporation for the period 1570-86[42] – covering John Shakespeare's time of high office. Additionally, Rogers was one of John Shakespeare's business partners[43], and therefore formed a direct link between Sir Thomas Lucy, and John Shakespeare's son, William. (He has the additional interest for Shakespeare scholars of being the coroner at Katherine Hamlet's inquest – she was drowned in 1579 and may have been a model for Ophelia.) But the web of connections ran even further; Fripp, writing of the Sommerville plot in 1583, tells us:

> "On 25 October [1583] John Somerville of Edstone, a young squire, late at Oxford, now married Margaret Arden, a kinswoman of Shakespeare's mother, daughter of Edward and Mary Arden of Park hall, fired by the fanaticism of the Ardens and their priest, Hugh Hall, set out from his house, six miles north of Stratford, for London, with the intention of shooting the heretical Queen. He was arrested next day . . . [and] conveyed to the Tower . . . on the 2 November the Clerk of the Privy Council, Thomas Wilkes, arrived at Charlecote and took Master and Mistress Arden prisoners. Thence, with Lucy . . . he proceeded to Edward Grant's house, Northbrook, in Snitterfield . . . Henry Rogers, who lived in Sherburn, Town Clerk of Stratford and agent of Sir Thomas Lucy, assisted the latter and Wilkes in their search for incriminating 'books and writings'."[44]

Fripp was wrong in stating that Northbrook was in Snitterfield: although adjoining it, it was in the parish of Fulbrook. It is highly ironic that having had a business connection with Grant regarding the purchase of Fulbrook, Lucy and Rogers should have raided his Northbrook house in search of incriminating Catholic literature: particularly as their business partner – John Sommerville – was the father of the main culprit in the conspiracy. This web of connections can only be clarified through further work.

Given that Lucy was listed as one of the purchasers of Fulbrook in the 1573 licence, and his family's involvement with the park, it is probable that he did acquire an interest in the estate. There is however, uncertainty as to what happened to Fulbrook after the 1570's. The crown appear to have ceased collecting rent from the estate after about 1575, although they continued to collect the rents from other land owned by Englefield.[45] A special act of parliament was passed in 1593, "An Acte for explanation and confirmaytion of the Queens Maiestes title to the lands and tenements late Sir Francis Englefields Knight attainted for high treason", and included in the confirmed lands was "the reversion and remainder of the parke called Fullbroke parke in the sayde Countie of Warwike."[46] The phrase "reversion and remainder" may refer to Margaret Englefield's interest in the property, for when it was leased to Nicholas Ffaunt, one of the Clerks of the Signet, in 1607, it was stated that the lease was "to begin after the death of Margaret Englefield who hath an estate in the said lands for term of her life."[47]

However, when the land was sold in 1610 to Sir William Willoughby and William Brock by the crown, it was sold in fee simple, but, "on composition for defective title".[48] What the basis of this "defective title" was, is unknown; it may refer to the chequered entanglements between the Englefields and the crown, but it also might relate to other transactions – such as that in the 1573 licence – involving the land previous to its sale in 1610. The Englefields had contested the right of the crown to their lands through the device of internal transfer, and this would have affected any grants the crown made of these lands – including the transfer of Fulbrook to Sir Thomas Lucy – before the special act of parliament in 1593.

There is evidence that Fulbrook was re-emparked at some date before 1588 (this will be discussed in the next chapter), and this seems to have taken place during the year 1573. In 1557, Fulbrook was described as "now disparked", with "all the woods sold and the pale taken awaye"; it consisted of 21 acres of meadow, 80 acres of pasture, and 400 acres of heath and wasteland.[49] In the inquisition of 19 June 1573, it was described as consisting of "1 messuage, 20 acres of meadow, 350 acres of pasture and 1 acre of woodland there called Fulbrook Park at £10 p.a.", whereas four months later on the 17th October it had expanded to "one messuage, twenty acres of meadow, 350 acres of pasture and 100 hundred acres woods called Fulbroke Park . . . value £40 per annum."[50] This latter description was used in all legal transactions right up to that used for the sale of the property to Willoughby and Brock in 1610, and the inclusion of woods in the property and the evidence to be considered in the next chapter, suggest it was being used as a deer park throughout most of this period. Sir Thomas Lucy's withdrawal of his two keepers from Hatton in the middle of 1574, indicates that the deer from Fulbrook ceased to roam over neighbouring ground, presumably because the estate had been re-emparked. (This might also explain his interest in acquiring the estate in April 1573.)

Fulbrook was only a mile or so away from Snitterfield, as was Ingon – both places with direct Shakespeare connections. Shakespeare's uncle,

Henry, farmed land at both Snitterfield and Ingon (his children were baptised in Hampton Lucy church), and John Shakepseare had in 1570 leased fourteen acres of land in Ingon, possibly that farmed by his brother Henry. But all these facts are irrelevant unless we can establish that there were deer parks at Fulbrook and Charlecote during the period that Shakespeare is alleged to have poached deer from Sir Thomas Lucy. What we need is a map – a map which shows deer parks in the mid-1580's – and to our great good fortune, such a map does exist, giving detail of parks and the area in which they were set.

CHAPTER 10: THE DEER PARK AND CONY WARREN AT CHARLECOTE

At some time in the middle of the sixteenth century, William Sheldon, a prosperous landowner in Warwickshire and Worcestershire, set up a tapestry-weaving industry on his estates at Beoley and Barcheston in Warwickshire.[1] In 1570, Sheldon left the weaving business to his son Ralph, along with money and grants to continue it. In Sheldon's will, there is mention of Richard Hicks, his manager at Barcheston, who may well have been trained in tapestry weaving and design in the Low Countries.

In 1588, Ralph Sheldon built himself a new mansion at Weston, near Long Compton in Warwickshire, and commissioned a set of four tapestry maps covering the counties of Warwickshire, Worcestershire, Oxfordshire with Berkshire, and Gloucestershire. According to the seventeenth century antiquary, Anthony Wood, these hung in the dining room of Weston, and were probably woven for Ralph Sheldon's new house. Not all the maps in this original series have survived, and a second set were woven some time after 1647 (one of them included the arms of Ralph Sheldon the younger impaling those of his wife whom he married in 1647), probably to replace the worn first set. In this second set was included a map of Warwickshire, bearing the date 1588; it was obviously not woven at this date because it incorporated Ralph Sheldon the younger's coat of arms, and a mid-seventeenth century style of borders. But given that the cartographical portions of the maps common to both series are identical, and that the second set all bear the date of 1588, it is clear that the second set is a copy of the first.

In fact, both editions of the map of Worcestershire have survived and are currently hanging in the *Victoria and Albert Museum*. This particular map includes that part of Warwickshire covering the Charlecote/ Fulbrook area, and the map of the first series, although not dated, has the name of Richard Hicks as its designer, and has a typical Elizabethan border for its surrounds. This map, although not complete, is in excellent condition where it has survived, and unlike the Warwickshire map itself, is laid out on a correct geographical basis, i.e. it was designed and woven so that north faced north, east – east etc. And this map seems remarkably accurate as far as distances and locations are concerned, as the reader will see from comparing Plate 3 with Plate 4. As Humphreys has observed in his book on the Sheldon tapestries, "the tapestry maps . . . suggest a personal knowledge of the county by the designer of each map, for usually the churches are correctly represented, with or without the spire."[2] This can be seen for example in Stratford : the two churches of that town are very accurately portrayed (see Plates 5 and 6). Barcheston, where the map was woven, is about ten miles from Charlecote, and there was a particular reason why the Sheldon weavers would have been familiar with Charlecote: William Sheldon had leased "the manors of Hampton Lucy and Hatton" from Sir Thomas Lucy, and the lease had only been re-assigned back to Lucy in 1573.[3]

The Sheldon tapestry map of Worcestershire bears very close scrutiny. The reader will notice that there is a paling attached to Charlecote, and that this is bounded on one side by the river Avon. What is not clear from a first reading of this map is the location of Fulbrook Park; there appears to be a park at "Wasburton" just east of Snitterfield, but no sign of Fulbrook. In fact what has happened is that the tapestry weavers took the location of Wasperton (Wasburton) from Saxton's 1576 map of Warwickshire, as did a number of subsequent mapmakers – rather than on the left-hand side of the river it should be on the right. (See Plate 4) Given that the rest of the Sheldon map is so accurate in detail – for example both the churches at Bishops Hampton and Wasperton are correctly depicted – it is surprising that this mistake was made. Saxton's map had such authority with contemporaries, that the Sheldon mapmakers preferred to believe that rather than the evidence of their own eyes.

If Wasperton is relocated in its correct position on the right side of the river, a park emerges exactly where Fulbrook was located. (See Plate 7) The Warwick to Stratford road runs alongside its paling, where Rous's robbers lay in waiting, and it is precisely where it should be according to the various descriptions of its location already discussed – in particular Leland's account already quoted : "I roade from Warwicke to Bareford

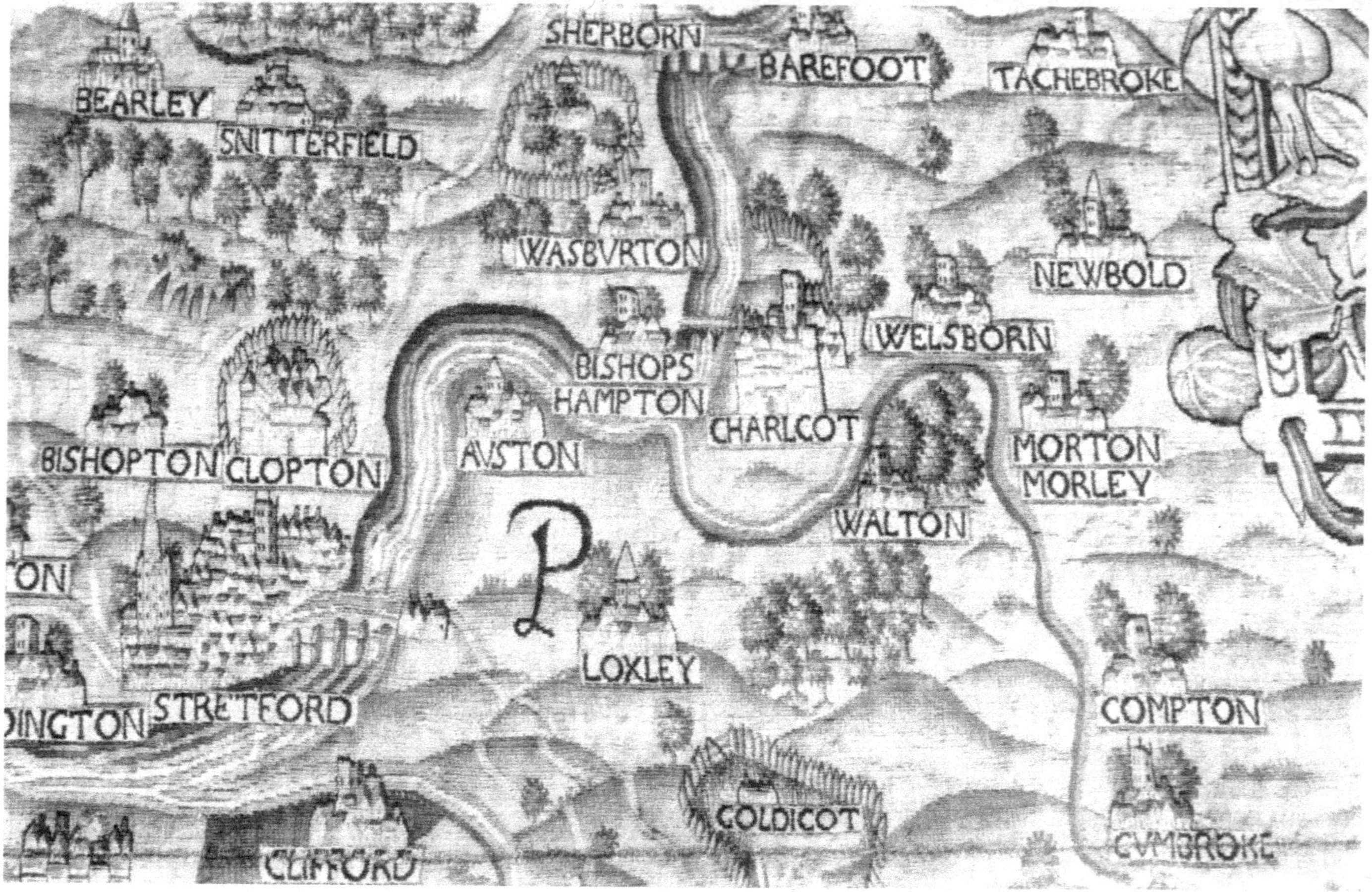

Plate 3: Charlecote and Surrounding Area (From Sheldon Tapestry Map of Worcestershire in The Victoria and Albert Museum)

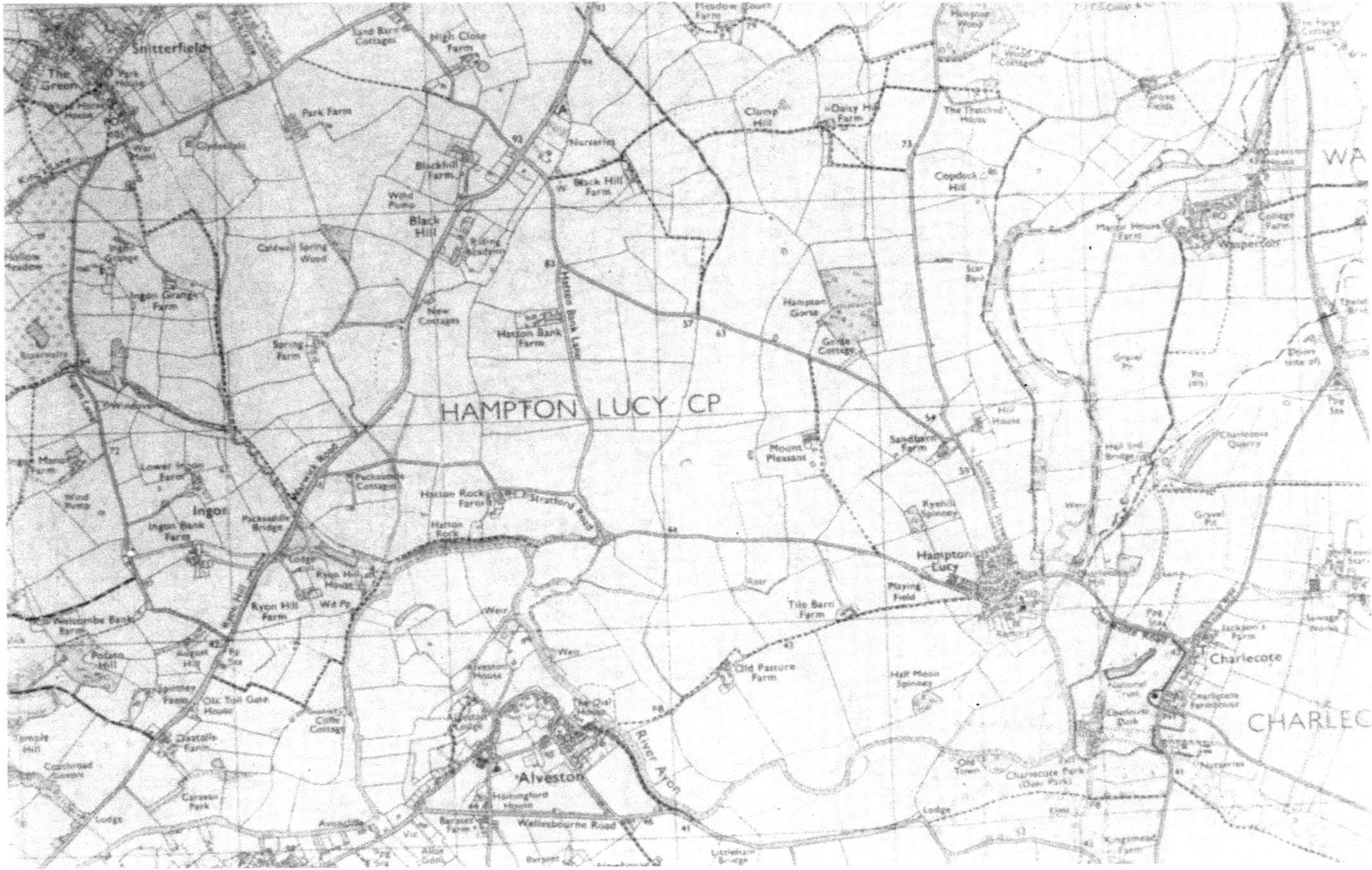

Plate 4: Charlecote and Surrounding Area, Ordnance Survey Map

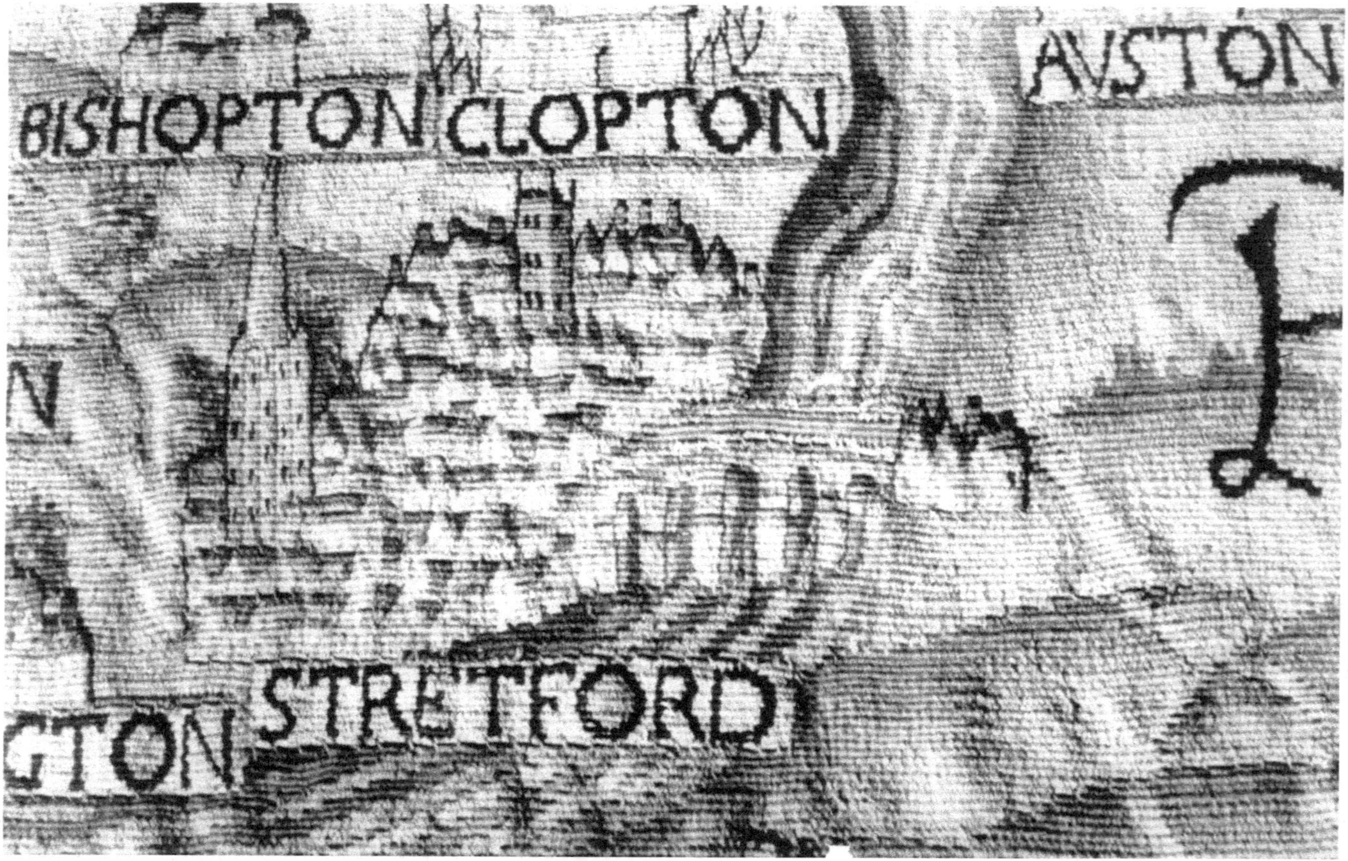

Plate 5: Stratford-On-Avon (From Sheldon Tapestry Map of Worcestershire in The Victoria and Albert Museum)

Plate 6: "View of Stratford-On-Avon" (From R. B. Wheeler, History and Antiquities of Stratford-On-Avon *[1806]).*

Plate 7: Fulbrook Park (From Sheldon Tapestry Map of Worcestershire in The Victoria and Albert Museum)

Bridge of 8 fayre arches a 2 miles [from Warwicke]. Here I sawe halfe a mile lower upon Avon on the right ripe by northe a fayr parke caulled Fulbroke." Also the detailed map of the area drawn up by Fish and and reproduced in Plate 2 confirms the identity of this park as Fulbrook. And so in 1588, about the time that Shakepeare is said to have poached deer and rabbits from Charlecote and deer from Fulbrook, we have documented evidence for the existence of parks in those places. The evidence for Fulbrook has been considered in some detail, and all we need to note at this point is the Sheldon map's confirmation of the proximity of the park to Snitterfield and Ingon where Shakespeare's Uncle Henry farmed land.

The picture for Charlecote is more complicated and I hope to be able to show that it was highly likely that there were deer in Sir Thomas Lucy's Charlecote park. The first thing to note is that the paling at Charlecote ran from the bridge at Bishops Hampton (Hampton Lucy) to Charlecote House, and then round in a semi-circle for about a mile up to the river. (See Plate 8) Bracebridge in his book about Shakespeare and his deer-stealing activites (written in 1862), tells us that "Sir Thomas Lucy, who in 1558 rebuilt the manor house of Charlecote as it now stands, imparked a considerable tract around it, on the left bank of the Avon in 1563 ...[which] ran along the bank of the Avon for nearly a mile."[4] This description fits perfectly with the Sheldon map – the Charlecote paling is shown ending just opposite Wasperton, which is about a mile north of Hampton Lucy. The only scholar to previously notice the significance of this paling was Fripp. Unfortunately he relied on the copy of the less accurate Warwickshire map, which shows a paling between the Avon and the Dene, a stream running between Charlecote and the village of Wellesbourne. He observed:

> "In the interesting tapestry-map of Warwickshire, woven at Barcheston in 1588, all that is visible of a park at Charlecote is on the left bank of the Avon, marked by a paling on the north-east of the house connecting the Avon with the Dene, the stream from Wellesbourne. Such an enclosure might serve for mares and foals – not for deer, which would soon be over the water inflicting damage on crops and pasture."[5]

Fripp did not seem to be aware of the Worcestershire map which showed the area in more accurate geographical detail; if he had examined this carefully, and walked over the territory opposite the Charlecote enclosure, he would have observed "Scar Bank" – a ridge running from Hampton Lucy bridge, right up to the bend in the river adjoining Grove

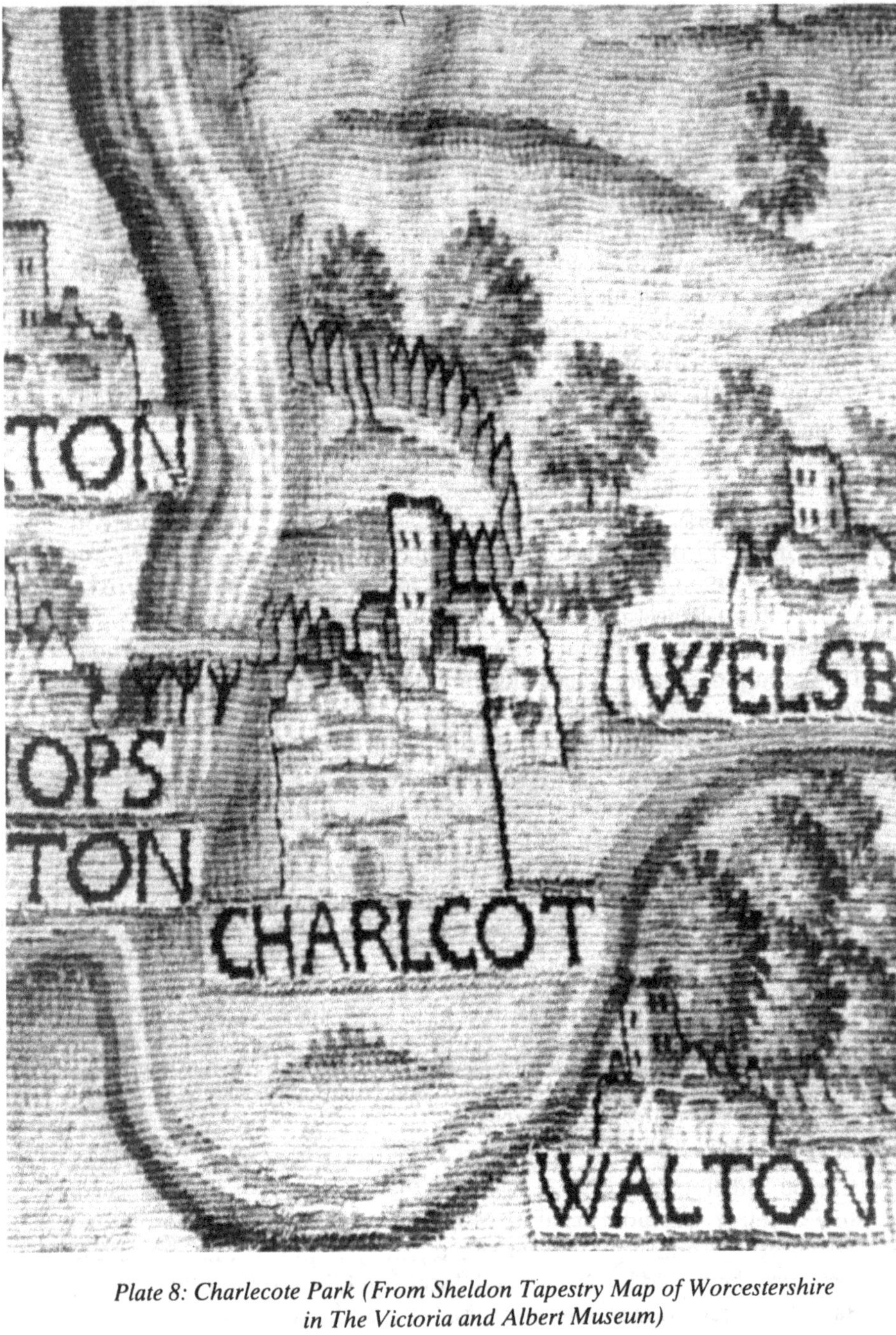

Plate 8: Charlecote Park (From Sheldon Tapestry Map of Worcestershire in The Victoria and Albert Museum)

Field. (See Plate 9). This bank forms a natural barrier on the other side of the river, and is fronted on both sides of the river by ground that even today is likely to flood, and probably in Shakespeare's day was largely marshland. Croom has observed of such a habitat: "Where the local topography allowed, natural boundaries such as a river or marshy ground might circumscribe the park."[6] In fact, the Worcestershire map shows a number of parks using a river as a part of its boundary: see for example the park at Strensham in Plate 10.

The river at Charlecote would have functioned partly to keep poachers out of the park, but also, depending on the ground, as a deterrent against the deer escaping the park grounds. Although deer swim readily, they will only do so if there is an incentive for good feed, and where there is not difficult marshy ground to traverse. We have already noticed that landowners only very rarely registered their deer parks, and Croom has observed that frequently "a small landowner received a grant of a free warren years before enclosing a deer park."[7] She noted that "the main purpose of a deer park was for hunting both for sport and for a supply of fresh meat . . . parks were also stocked with smaller game, including hares, rabbits, partridges and pheasants, which were an additional source of meat for the household."[8] (See Plate 11).

Sir Thomas Lucy always used the term "keeper", not "warrener" for the men responsible for the game in his park; and it is revealing that William Hullett had come as keeper from Hatton to head-keeper at Charlecote, suggesting deer-keeping was one of his main responsibilities. But undoubtedly Lucy's park was used for storing rabbits, and it is likely that these were hunted along with the other game in the enclosure. As one authority on rabbits has noted, "Hawking is . . . a very satisfactory way of taking rabbits . . . [and] twenty or more rabbits can be taken in a day" through this method.[9] As we have previously noted, Sir Thomas Lucy kept at least one falconer at Charlecote and it is likely that a part of their duties was the hunting of rabbits.

It was not uncommon for parks to be stocked with both deer and rabbits; for example, during the survey of Richard Norton's lands at Ripon in 1570, it was noted that "within half a mile of his house, he has a park of 1 miles, well stored with deer and conies, which are now nearly spoiled."[10] We have already seen that Charlecote was "imparked" at the end of the fifteenth century, and that there is evidence that deer were kept there in about 1520. The enclosure depicted in the Sheldon tapestry map, and described by Bracebridge, was far too extensive to be used merely for

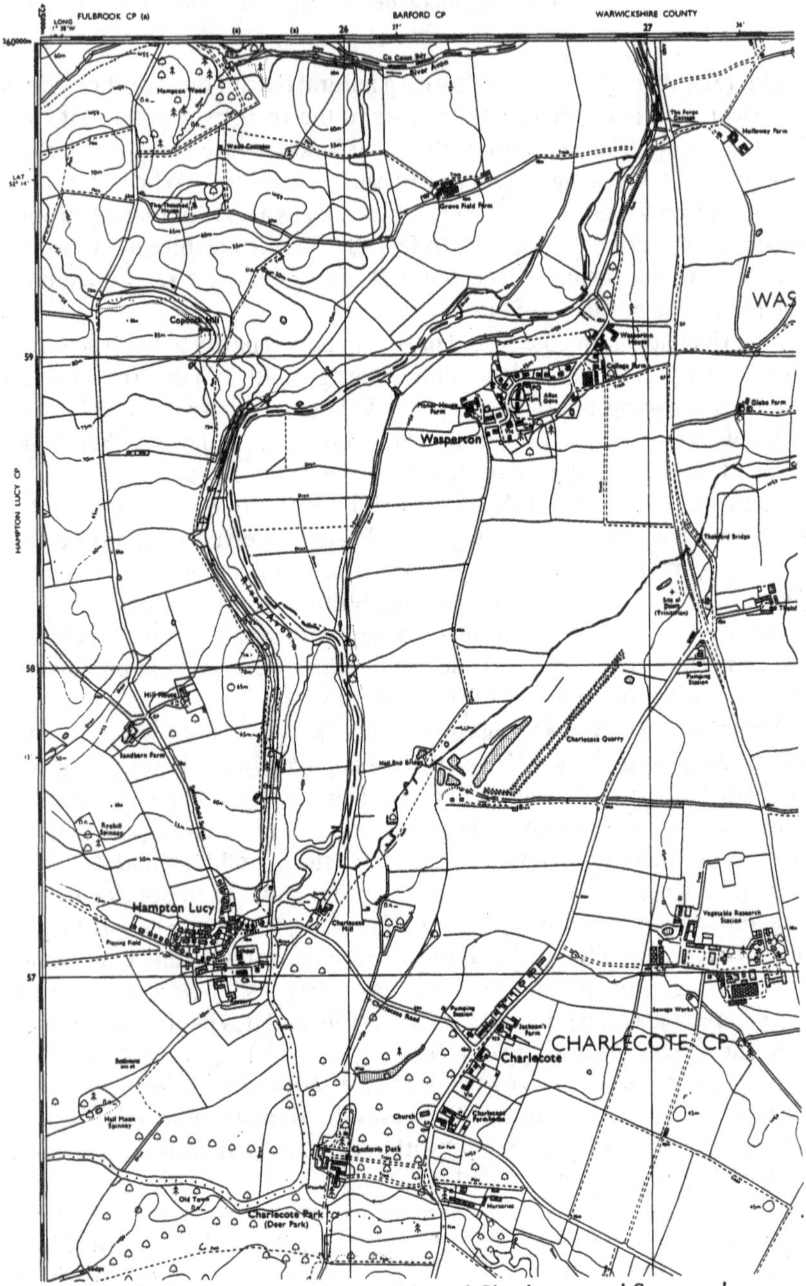

Plate 9: Ordnance Survey Map of Charlecote and Surrounds

Plate 10: Strensham Park (From Sheldon Tapestry Map of Worcestershire in The Victoria and Albert Museum)

Plate 11: "Deer Park and Cony Warren" (Tapestry, in The Victoria and Albert Museum)

the stocking of rabbits. Evidence that it was used as a park as well as a warren is provided by two leases made for ground in Charlecote in the mid-seventeenth century. In March 1663 a lease was granted by Richard Lucy to Richard Hinton and Robert Sandys, "husbandmen . . . of Charlecote", to farm land described as follows:

> "All that pasture ground or ground inclosed commonly called the parke situate lieing and being in Charlecote aforesayd & adjoyning to the Mansion house of the sayd Richard Lucy... except . . . All trees whatsoever . . . with full power & authority [for Lucy] with his . . . servants . . . to fell cut downe and carry away the same . . . [but the tenants to maintain] the gates railes hedges ditches mounds & fences."[11]

The lease was to run for four years, at a rent of £40 a year. This was exactly the same rental value that Fulbrook Park was valued at during the late sixteenth and early seventeenth century, which gives an idea of the extent of the old Charlecote Park. The land was further leased in 1679, with some additional detail in its description; the lands leased contained "the two partes of the parke wherein the pooles are situate and being in the Parish of Charlecott . . . [except] Woods and Underwoods, timber trees and other trees hedges and hedged Bowds whatsoever now standing growing . . . or being upon the said Demised Premises."[12] There are virtually no woods left now in this area, although from the descriptions in the leases, there seems to have been extensive woodland during the first half of the seventeenth century. (In 1598, Abraham Sturley, in a letter to Richard Quiney, referred to Sir Thomas Lucy as one of the "knightes of the woodland".) The park as described ran north from Charlecote House up to Charlecote Quarry; it was contained within the parish of Charlecote and so would not have been as extensive as the old park depicted in the Sheldon Tapestry Map. The latter ran up to the river – presumably where the river and Scar Bank joined – which is almost exactly opposite Wasperton, the location indicated by the tapestry map. Presumably Sir Thomas Lucy rented this extra ground from the owner of the manor of Wasperton, in whose jurisdiction it lay.

It should be noted that the join of the river with Scar Bank is adjacent to Grovefield and very near to the site of the old deer-barn; the latter lies between Fulbrook Park and the old Charlecote Park, so it is possible that Shakespeare hid here after poaching from either of these parks. However, he would have had to have crossed the river to get into Charlecote at this location – possible but more difficult than entering Fulbrook, which lay directly adjacent to the deer barn.

There is the question of the punishment that was meted out to Shakespeare as a result of his poaching activities; scholars have previously noted that as Charlecote was a warren rather than a park, Shakespeare could not have been punished for poaching deer from there. (This objection would obviously not apply to Fulbrook, which was a registered deer park). In order to meet this critical point, we must examine the relevant legislation of the period. In 1563 it was enacted that "if any person or persons . . . break or enter into any park impaled, or any other several ground closed with wall, pale or hedge, and used for the keeping, breeding, and cherishing of deer, and so wrongfully hunt, drive or chase out, or take, kill, or slay any deer . . . shall suffer imprisonment . . . of three months, and shall yield & pay to the party grieved his treble damages." But the Act then went on to stipulate that it did not apply "to any park or enclosed ground heereafter to be made and used for deer, without the grant or licence of our sovereign lady the Queen."[13] The Act gave protection to an enclosure which was used as a deer park by "immemorial prescription", and this was crucial, because as we have seen, less than ten per cent of deer parks were licenced. Also the distinction made by the law between parks and warrens was a very ambiguous one, as was shown by legislation enacted in 1540:

> "if any p[er]son . . . wrongefully take kill or slee any Deere within any parke or closed ground used for Deere, or with any hay or other nette or with any fyrett or pursenett any of the conyes or rabettis being within any parke or ground closed for maynten'nce or keping of Deere, or in any place being laufull warren . . . shalbe adjudged and taken felony; and that thoffendeer and offendours therein being thereof laufully attaynted shalhave and suffre suche paynes of death and shall lose and fofaicte theer goodis and cattalle landis and tenements . . . Provided always that this acte or any thing therein conteyn'd extend not to any park or inclosed grounde used for Deere, heretofore had or made without the graunt or lycence . . . or otherwise not allowed or approved of recorde; nor to any grounde herafter to be impark'd or inclosid for Deere by any of the Kinges subjectis, nor to any groundes not nowe usid as a warren for or of any conyes at this present tyme."[14]

The legislation of 1563 made no reference to the 1540 Act, and so the provisions of the latter, where they were not superceded by the former, were still in force by Shakespeare's time. In particular, the provisions relating to warrens – including the very severe punishments – would have applied to the poaching of rabbits. The 1540 Act was rather ambiguous in its definition of a park or a warren: it certainly protected rabbits kept in a deer park; but it is less clear whether deer kept in a licenced warren were also protected. The Act appears to have envisaged parks and warrens as overlapping in their functions, which is entirely consistent with what we know of the history of Charlecote.

Davies in his account of the poaching tradition states that Shakespeare was "oft whipt & sometimes imprisoned", and although legislation stipulated imprisonment, nowhere does it mention whipping. However, it was notorious during Shakespeare's time that magistrates were a law unto themselves; for example, Lambard complained in 1582 "that justices of the peace . . . arrogate unto themselves authority to use their discretion, and to play, as it were, the Chancellor in every cause that cometh before them."[15] Sir Robert Cecil was even more specific in a letter he wrote in 1600: "for my deare that are killed, what I can do by law I will prove, but otherwise I will reveng myself by no other meanes under color of authority being in myne owne case"[16] – exactly the position of Sir Thomas Lucy, justice of the peace.

That whipping was seen by contemporaries as a minor form of punishment, is indicated by one author's satirical observation of the effects of a free-school education: "I must needs come short of their experience that are bred up in free-schools, who, by plotting to rob an orchard,etc, run . . . under no higher penalty than a whipping."[17] All in all, contemporary legislation and authority of magistrates, gave Sir Thomas Lucy all the power that he needed to very harshly punish the young Shakespeare. All the ingredients of the poaching tradition are to be found in the historical record: two areas of enclosed parkland, a registered deer park (Fulbrook) and cony warren (Charlecote), a gatehouse, estate game-keepers, the presence of both deer and rabbit in at least one of Sir Thomas Lucy's parks, and the existence of legislation stipulating severe punishment for poaching. The weight of evidence therefore supports the various traditional accounts of Shakespeare's deer and cony-stealing exploits – sometimes in great detail – and that by breaking into the park, he incurred the wrath of Sir Thomas Lucy and was forced to flee to London to avoid further punishment.

CHAPTER 11: THE WILD YOUTH

In all, there are mentions of deer-hunting and cony-catching in eighteen of Shakespeare's plays and two in his narrative poems: *The Comedy Of Errors*, *The Winter's Tale*, *Cymbeline*, *King Henry VI*, *As You Like It*, *Love's Labour's Lost*, *Coriolanus*, *Much Ado About Nothing*, *The Merry Wives Of Windsor*, *Anthony And Cleopatra*, *Hamlet*, *Macbeth*, *Julius Caesar*, *The Taming Of The Shrew*, *Twelth Night*, *Troilus And Cressida*, *Titus Andronicus*, *Romeo And Juliet*, *Venus And Adonis*, and *The Rape Of Lucrece*. If interpreted correctly, these references can make a significant contribution to Shakespeare biography. A passage from *The Winter's Tale* enables us to estimate the approximate date that Shakespeare was involved in the poaching incident. The old shepherd, hearing his sons hunting, laments:

> "I would there no age betweene ten and three and twenty, or that youth would sleep out the reste; for there is nothing (in the betweene) but getting wenches with childe, wronging the Auncientry, stealing, fighting, hearke you now: would any but these boylde-braines of nineteene, and two and twenty hunt this weather?"[1]

Shakespeare was born approximately in April 1564 and his younger brother, Gilbert, in October 1566. In the summer of 1586, William would have been twenty-two, and his brother nineteen; the shepherd tells us that the wildness of youth ends at the age of twenty-three. Although purely speculative, if this passage were read to apply to Shakespeare, this would give a date of 1587 for the year he was caught poaching Lucy's deer. Echoes of the relationship between the shepherd and his two sons are found in the relationship between Belarius and his two adopted sons Guiderius and Arviragus, in *Cymberline*. Arviragus laments his impoverished and narrow provincial circumstances:

"What thing is't, that I neuer/ Did see man dye, scarse euer look'd on blood,/ But that of Coward Hares, hot Goats , and Venison?/ Neuer bestrid a Horse saue one, that had/ A Rider like my selfe, who ne'er wore Rowell/ Nor Iron on his heele? I am asham'd/ To looke vpon the holy Sunne, to haue/ The benefit of his blest Beames, remaining/ So long a poore vnknowne."[2]

It is possible to see here expressions of what Shakespeare called in Sonnet 121 "my sportive blood". There is sufficient detail in the plays to give us some idea of the setting and the method used by Shakespeare in his poaching activities. In one of his first plays, *King Henry VI*, "park'd and bounded in a pale – A little herd of England's timorous deer", where the King stood "close to steale the Bishop's Deere"[3], the scene is set in "A chase in the north of England":

"*Enter Sinklo, and Humfrey, with Crosse-bowes in their hands.*
Sinklo Vnder this thicke growne brake, wee'l shrowd our selues:/ For through this Laund anon the Deere will come,/ And in this couert will we make our Stand,/ Culling the principall of all the Deere.
Humfrey Ile stay aboue the hill, so both may shoot.
Sinklo That cannot be, the noise of thy Crosse-bow/ Will scarre the Heard, and so my shot is lost:/ Heere stand we both, and ayme we at the best ..."[4]

This scene is reminiscent of that in *Love's Labour's Lost*, where standing in the park, the forester tells the princess in order to kill the deer, she must place herself "vpon the edge of yonder Coppice,/ A Stand where you may make the fairest shoote."[5] The actual death of the deer is described in *As You Like It*, in the setting of the Forest of Arden:

"Vnder an oake, whose anticke roote peepes out/ Vpon the brooke that brawles along this wood,/ To the which place a poore sequestred Stag,/ That from the hunter's aime had tane a hurt,/ Did come to languish; and indeed my Lord,/ The wretched animall heau'd forth such groanes/ That their discharge did stretch his leatherne coat/ Almost to bursting, and the big round teares/ Cours'd one another downe his innocent nose/ In pitteous chase: and thus the hairie foole,/ Much marked of the melancholie *Jacques*,/ Stood on th' extremest verge of the swift brooke,/ Augmenting it with teares."[6]

This is reminiscent of Benedick's comment on the Count in *Much Ado About Nothing*: "I found him heere as melancholy as a Lodge in a Warren."[7] That Shakespeare was familiar with conies is shown by his references to them in *Coriolanus* – "they will out of their Burroughes, (like Conies after Raine)"[8] – and *King Henry VI* – "So doth the Connie struggle in the Net."[9] And there is a touch of his own experience in his satire on Master Slender: "he is as tall a man of his hands, as any is betweene this and his head: he hath fought with a Warrener."[10] That all forms of game could be hunted in one area of parkland is revealed in one of Shakespeare's first published writings, *Venus And Adonis*:

> "But if thou needs wilt hunt, be rul'd by me;/ Uncouple at the timorous flying hare,/ Or the fox which lives by subtlety,/ Or at the roe which no encounter dare . . . And when thou hast on foot the purblind hare,/ Mark the poor wretch . . . Sometimes he runs . . . where earth-delving conies keep,/ To stop the loud pursuers in their yell;/ And sometimes sorteth with a herd of deer."

Shakespeare was very familiar with the terms used by sportsmen for the different categories of deer; in *Love's Labour's Lost*, he makes the following play on words: "The prayfull Princesse pearst and prickt a prettie pleasing Pricket,/ Some say a Sore, but not a sore till now made sore with shooting./ The Dogges did yell, put ell to Sore, then Sorell jumps from thicket:/ Or Pricket sore, or else Sorell, the people fall a hooting./ If Sore be sore, then ell to Sore, makes fiftie sores O sorell:/ Of one sore I an hundred make by adding but one more L."[11] A pricket is a stag in its second year, a sorell is one in its third year, and a sore one in its fourth year.

Shakespeare invariably uses the language of the hunt metaphorically. Anthony laments Caesar's fate in just such a fashion: "Heere was't thou bay'd braue Hart . . . O World! thou wast the Forrest to this Hart . . . How like a Deere, stroken by many Princes,/ Dost thou heere lye."[12] Similarly, after lamenting the fate of the wounded stag, Jacques exclaims: "Sweepe on you fat and greazie Citizens,/ 'Tis just the fashion:/ wherefore doe you looke/ Vpon that poore and broken bankrupt there?"[13] As well as a metaphor of violence, Shakespeare frequently uses the pursuit and hunting of deer as a sexual metaphor: "Oh thus I found her straying in the Parke,/ Seeking to hide herselfe as doth the Deare/ That hath receiued some vnrecuring wound."[14] And the winning of woman and the stealing of deer were directly juxtaposed:

> "Why, mak'st thou it so strange?/ Shee is a woman, therefore may be woo'd,/ Shee is a woman, therefore may be wone . . . Then why should he dispaire that knowes to court it/ With words, faire lookes, and liberality:/ What hast not thou full often strucke a Doe,/ And borne her cleanly by the Keepers nose?"[15]

Sometimes the language is playfully possessive: "Within the circuit of this ivory pale,/ I'll be a park, and thou shalt be my deer . . . Then be my deer, since I am such a park;/ No dog shall rouse thee, though a thousand bark."[16] Other times the language is more violent, as in the *Twelfth Night:* "O when mine eyes did see *Olivia* first,/ Me thought she purg'd the ayre of pestilence;/ That instant was I turn'd into a Hart,/ And my desires like fell and cruell hounds,/ Ere since pursue me."[17] Hunting and sexuality were inextricably linked in Shakespeare's mind, and of the many quotes we could select to illustrate this, perhaps the most apt – although with a touch of Oedipus – is from one of his early narrative poems:

> "She hearkens for his hounds and for his horn./ Anon she hears them chant it lustily./ And all in haste she coasteth to the cry./ And as she runs, the bushes in the way/ Some catch her by the neck, some kiss her face,/ Some twine about her thigh to make her stay;/ She wildly breaketh from their strict embrace,/ Like a milk doe whose swelling dugs do ache/ Hasting to feed her fawn hid in some brake."[18]

★ ★ ★

Underlying Shakespeare's treatment of violence and sex, there lies a general theme of the wildness of youth. In *Hamlet*, Polonius complains of "such wanton, wild, and vsual slips,/ As are Companions noted and most knowne/ To youth and liberty."[19] This wildness was seen by Shakespeare as mainly physical: "Young bloud doth not obey an old decree"[20] – although, "The bloud of youth burns not with such excesse/ As grauity's reuolt to wantons be."[21] Wildness was linked with rebellion: "Naturall rebellion, done i'th blade of youth,/ When oyle and fire, too strong for reasons force,/ Ore-beares it, and burnes on."[22] But "the aimes, and ends of burning youth" had to be curbed by custom and law: "We haue strict Statutes, and most biting Laws,/ The needfull bits and curbes to headstrong weedes."[23]

This rebellious wildness was often sexual: "In generall Riot, melted downe thy youth/ In different beds of Lust, and neuer learn'd/ The Icie precepts of respect, but followed/ The sugred game before thee."[24] Much of this can be related to Shakespeare's own experience; he was only eighteen when he married – his wife was eight years older – and his first child, Susanna was born less than six months after the date of his marriage.[25] Although there may have been a pre-marital contract between Shakespeare and Anne Hathaway, this type of contract had become rare by the 1580's.[26] This was reflected in the pattern of marriage in Stratford during this period: of 109 marriages which took place between 1580 and 1599, only 11.9% resulted in children born less than six months after marriage. (The figure increased to 17.4% for under eight months, and 29.3% for under eight-and-a-half months.)[27] Thus it was only a minority of marriages where the wife was pregnant at marriage, and this was particularly the case for brides who had been pregnant for three months or more.

Through recent research, it is also possible to throw light on the question of age of marriage: the mean age of first marriage for women in Stratford ranged between 21.1 and 25.6 years in the period 1580-1624, and for men the equivalent figures were 25.8 and 28.2. The samples for the earlier period are too small to be reliable, and if we aggregate them to reasonable sizes, we arrive at the following figures: the average age for women in 1580-1609 was 23.0 (based on a sample of 111 women), and men in 1590-1609 was 27.16 (a sample of 71).[28] This was very similar to what it was in the two neighbouring rural parishes of Wellesbourne and Alveston: for women 24.1 in 1595-1629, and men 27.8 – although Skipp found in his Forest of Arden parishes for the period 1575-99, mean ages of marriage of 26.3 for women and 29.7 for men.[29] Anne Hathaway came from a rural parish, and so perhaps the latter averages are more relevant to her. The conclusion from these various figures is that Anne Hathaway at twenty-six may have been a little older than the average woman when married, but not very much older – and certainly not the "older" woman that many previous biographers have labelled her. It is rather the the reverse which is true: Shakespeare was a lot younger than most of his contemporaries, who on average married ten years later than he did. Marrying at the age of eighteen must have been very rare (we do not have the exact figures), and probably was the result of Anne Hathaway being pregnant at the time of marriage.

Shakespeare was deeply ambivalent about pre-marital sexuality: on the one hand some passages in the plays indicate a belief in the morality of the pre-marital contract, whereas others, indicate strong moral disapproval. In *All's Well That Ends Well* (Act 5, Scene iii), Diana demands of Bertram, "Ask him vpon his oath, if hee do's thinke/ He had not my virginity" – to which Bertram replies : "certaine it is I lyk'd her,/ And boorded her i'th wanton way of youth." And Prospero warns Ferdinand against similar treatment of Miranda:

> "Worthily purchas'd, take my daughter: But/ If thou do'st breake her Virgin-knot, before/ All sanctimonious ceremonies may/ With full and holy right, be ministred,/ No sweet aspersion shall the heauens let fall/ To make

> this contract grow; but barraine hate,/ Sower-ey'd disdaine, and discord, shall bestrew/ The vnion of your bed, with weedes so loathly/ That you shall hate it both: Therefore take heede,/ As Hymens Lamps shall light you."[30]

This was written towards the end of Shakespeare's life, and probably his attitude had hardened as he got older. But the reflection of his own experience was to be found in Caliban, the embodiment – to use Jung's phrase – of Prospero's "shadow" ("this Thing of darknesse, I/ Acknowledge mine"[31]): "Thou most lying slaue,/ Whom stripes may moue, not kindnes: I haue vs'd thee/ (Filth as thou art) with humane care, and lodg'd thee/ In mine owne Cell, till thou didst seek to violate/ The honor of my childe."[32]

The change in Shakespeare's attitude is reflected in the clown's song in *Hamlet:* "In youth when I did loue, did loue,/ me thought it was very sweete:/ To contract O the time for a my behoue,/ O me thought there was nothing meete . . . But Age with his stealing steps/ hath caught me in his clutch:/ And hath shipped me intill the Land,/ as if I had neuer beene such."[33] But the idea of a linear shift of attitude is too simple; Shakespeare's characters declaim varying attitudes in different plays, with no obvious chronology. In one of the earliest plays, *Love's Labour's Lost*, the Princess protests by her "maiden honor, yet as pure/ As the vnsallied Lilly"[34], whereas in a play of the middle period, *Twelth Night*, reference is made to "A Contract of eternall bond of loue,/ Confirm'd by mutuall joynder of your hands,/ Attested by the holy close of lippes,/ Strengthned by enterchangement of your rings,/ And all the Ceremonie of this compact."[35]

The ambiguity of attitude is reflected directly in a number of passages; when Claudio casts aspersions on Hero's honour as "a maid", Leonato rejoins, "Deere my Lord, if you in your owne proofe,/ Haue vanquisht the resistance of her youth,/ And made defeat of her virginitie" – to which Claudio interrupts: "I know what you would say: if I haue knowne her,/ You will say, she did imbrace me as a husband,/ And so extenuate the forehand sinne."[36] And perhaps the young Shakespeare's impatience can be seen in Rosalind's speech in *As You Like It:* "Marry he trots hard with a yong maid, between the contract of her marriage, and the day it is solemnizd: if the interim be but a sennight, Time's pace is so hard, that it seemes the length of seuen yeare."[37]

The play which deals mainly with the issue of the morality of pre-marital conception is *Measure For Measure*. The theme is treated in such a complex fashion that it is impossible to do justice to it here as part of a more general discussion. Suffice it to say, that the same ambiguity and ambivalence noted elsewhere, is also to be found in this play. This can be illustrated by quoting from Act 1, Scene 2; Claudio is to be sent to prison "for getting Madam *Julietta* with childe". Claudio engages in dialogue with Lucio about the morality of the issue

> "*Claudio* Thus can the demy god (Authority)/ Make vs pay downe, for our offence, by waight/ The words of heauen; on whom it will, it will/ On whom it will not, (soe) yet still 'tis just.
> *Lucio* Why how now *Claudio:* whence comes this restraint.
> *Claudio* From too much liberty, my *Lucio* Liberty/ As surfet is the father of much fast,/ So euery Scope by the immoderate vse/ Turnes to restraint: Our natures do pursue/ Like rats that rauyn downe their proper Bane,/ A thirsty euill; and when we drinke, we die.
> *Lucio* . . . what's thy offence, *Claudio?* . . . Lecherie?
> *Claudio* Call it so . . . vpon a true contract/ I got possession of *Julietas* bed./ You know the Lady, she is fast my wife,/ Save that we doe the denunciation lacke/ Of outward Order. This we came not to,/ Onely for propagation of a Dowre/ Remaining in the Coffer of her friends, From whom we thought it meet to hide our Loue/ Till Time had made them for vs. But it chances/ The stealth of our most mutuall entertainment/ With Character too grosse, is writ on *Juliet*."

What was the result of this ambiguity of attitude in Shakespeare's own life? The passage quoted earlier from *The Tempest* – "If thou do'st breake her Virgin-knot, before/ All sanctimonious ceremonies . . . barraine hate,/ Sowerr-ey'd disdaine, and discord shall bestrew/ The vnion of your bed ..." – suggests that Shakespeare's marriage was not a happy one. We will be looking later at other evidence in support of this conclusion – in particular the sonnets – but the fact that he mainly worked in London after he came to maturity, that he left his wife and children in Stratford, and only visited them, according to tradition, once a year[38], is certainly consistent with it.

Looking at his writings for a reflection of his attitude towards marriage, we see at the beginning a period of optimism: "To the best Bride-bed will we,/ Which by vs shall blessed be:/ And the issue there create/ Euer shall be fortunate:/ So shall all the couples three/ Ever true in louing be."[39] And during this early period, the "new married Wife about her Husbands Necke, [is] hardly to be shooke off"[40], and as long as marriage is rightly ordered, "peace it boads, and loue, and quiet life . . . And to be short, what not, that's sweete and happie."[41]

But very quickly things change: "men are Aprill when they woe, December when they wed"[42], and as one wife complains about husbands, "when you haue our Roses/ You barely leave our thornes to pricke our selues,/ And mocke vs with our barenesse."[43] And this is echoed in *Twelth Night* (2, iv), in a situation very similar to Shakespeare's own, of a very young man marrying an older woman. Addressing remarks to a young man/boy (Viola in disguise), the Duke advises: "Let still the woman take/ An elder than her selfe; so weares she to him;/ So swayes she leuell in her husbands heart:/ For boy, howeuer we do praise our seiues,/ Our fancies are more giddie and vnfirme,/ More longing, wauering, sooner lost and worne,/ Then womens are . . . Then let thy Loue be yonger then thy selfe,/ Or thy affection cannot hold the bent:/ For women are as Roses, whose fair flowre/ Being once displaid, doth fall that verie howre."

The play in which the theme of the internal disintegration of marriage is depicted, is *The Comedy Of Errors*. Through the device of mistaken identity, Shakespeare is able to indirectly explore tensions within marriage. The nature of the marriage between Antipholus and Adriana, although treated as a part of a comic plot, is revealed through the dialogue between the Abbess and Adriana:

> "*Abbess* Hath he not lost much wealth by wrack of sea,/ Buried some deere friend, hath not else his eye/ Stray'd his affection in vnlawfull loue,/ A sinne preuailing much in youthfull men/ Who giue their eies the liberty of gazing./ Which of these sorrowes is he subject to?
> *Adriane* To none of these, except it be the last;/ Namely, some loue that drew him oft from home.
> *Abbess* You should have for that haue reprehended him.
> *Adriane* Why so I did.
> *Abbess* I but not rough enough.
> *Adriane* As roughly as my modestie would let me.
> *Abbess* Haply in priuate.
> *Adriane* And in assemblies too.
> *Abbess* I, but not enough.
> *Adriane* It was the copie of our Conference./ In bed he slept not for my vrging it/ At boord he fed not for my vrging it:/ Alone, it was the subject of my Theame:/ In company I often glanced it:/ Still did I tell him, it was vilde and bad.
> *Abbess* And thereof came it, that the man was mad./ The venome clamors of a jealous woman,/ Poisons more deadly then a mad dogges tooth./ It seemes his sleepes were hindred by thy railing,/ And thereof comes it that his head is light./ Thou saist his meat was sawcd with thy vpbraidings,/ Vnquiet meales make ill digestions;/ Thereof the raging fire of feauer bred;/ And what's a Feauer, but a fit of madnesse?/ Thou sayest his sports were hindred by thy bralles./ Sweet recreation barr'd, what doth ensue/ But

moodie and dull melancholly,/ Kinsman to grim and comfortlesse dispaire."[44]

Antipholus's unfaithfulness is suggested earlier in the play: "My wife is shrewish when I keepe not howres . . . I know a wench of excellent discourse,/ Prettie and wittie; wilde, and yet too gentle;/ There we will dine . . . To her will we to dinner."[45] Luciana, Adriana's sister, upbraids Antipholus for his unfaithfulness: "Euen in the spring of Loue, thy Loue-springs rot? . . . if you like else-where, doe it by stealth,/ Muffle your false loue with some shew of blindnesse:/ Let my sister not read it in your eye . . . Be secret false: what need she be acquainted?/ . . . 'Tis double wrong to truant with your bed/ And let her read it in thy lookes at boord . . . Though others have the arm, show vs the sleeue."[46]

The wife's bitterness at this treatment is described through Emilia's speech in *Othello:* "Let Husbands know/ Their wiues have sense like them: They see, and smell,/ And haue their Palats both for sweet, and sowre/ As husbands haue. What is it that they do/ When they change vs for others? Is it Sport? I thinke it is: and doth Affection breed it?/ I thinke it doth. Is't Frailty that thus erres?/ It is so too. And haue we not Affections,/ Desires for Sport? and Frailty, as men haue?/ Then let them use vs well: else let them know,/ The illes we do, their illes instruct vs so."[47]

We should note that in this passage, as elsewhere, Shakespeare uses a sporting metaphor for sexual unfaithfulness. That the theme of unfaithfulness was not merely fictional, is indicated by the sonnets. His love for the dark lady and his fair friend are too familiar to warrant any extensive discussion. There are however sonnets which do illuminate the themes under discussion, and these will be briefly considered. In sonnet 152, Shakespeare confesses his unfaithfulness: "In loving thee thou know'st I am forsworn./ But thou art twice forsworn, to me love swearing;/ In act thy bed-vow broke, and new faith torn/ In vowing new hate after new love bearing./ But why of these two oaths' breach do I accuse thee,/ When I break twenty?" Earlier in sonnets 141 and 142, he was even more explicit: "Only my plague thus far I count my gain,/ That she that makes me sin awards me pain./ Love is my sin . . . those lips of thine . . . Robb'd others' beds' revenues of their rents."

And the sonnet following, sonnet 143, is perhaps the most self-revealing of all those written by Shakespeare. It is not within the brief of this book to analyse psychological motivation in detail – this has been undertaken by Freud, Jones and other psycho-analytical writers – but it is appropriate to briefly consider the relevance of some of this material. Sonnet 143 runs:

> "Lo as a careful huswife runs to catch/ One of her feathered creatures broke away,/ Sets down her babe, and makes all swift dispatch/ In pursuit of the thing she would have stay;/ Whilst her neglected child holds her in chase,/ Cries to catch her whose busy care is bent/ To follow that which flies before her face./ Not prizing her poor infant's discontent;/ So run'st thou after that which flies from thee,/ Whilst I thou babe chase thee afar behind;/ But if thou catch thou hope, turn back to me,/ And play the mother's part, kiss me, be kind./ So will I pray that thou mayst have thy Will,/ If thou turn back and my loud crying still."

The sonnet reveals a strong oedipal theme: the child/man is rejected by the mother/woman, leading to a desperate and dependent pleading for love – and it does not require a great deal of psychological understanding to see that the almost inevitable consequence is rejection, hurt and anger. Shakespeare's bitterness towards the dark lady had tinges of both sadism and masochism. The latter is dominant, and certainly when she appears as a figure in the plays, she usually is presented in that guise. In *Love's Labour's Lost*, Rosaline is described "as blacke as Ebonie . . . [and] Blacke is the badge of hell,/ The hue of dungeons, and the Schoole of night."[48] And likewise, in *Romeo And Juliet*, Mercutio, referring to another Rosaline, describes how "that same pale hard-harted wench, that *Rosaline*/ torments him so, that he sure will run mad."[49] And perhaps it is no co-incidence, that a character with virtually the same name – Rosalind – is, in *As You Like It*, associated with another dark lady, Celia: the shepherd falls in love with Celia's "foulnesse", and Celia falls in love with Rosalind's "anger".[50] Three dark ladies with the name of Rosaline/ Rosalind – is it possible that in real life, that Shakespeare's dark lady carried that name?

That Shakespeare was capable of dramatising his feelings towards the dark lady in inverted form is illustrated by the scene between Demetrius and Helena in *A Midsummer's Night Dream*. Helena declaims: "I am your spaniell, and *Demetrius*,/ The more you beat me, I will fawne on you./ Vse me but as your spaniell; spurne me, strike me,/ Neglect me, lose me; only giue me leave/ (Vnworthy as I am) to follow you./ What worser place can I beg in your loue,/ (And yet a placc of high respect for me)/ Then to be vsed as you doe your dogge?"[51] In view of this, it is perhaps not surprising that Shakespeare at times adopted a very misogynistic viewpoint, expressed most vividly in *King Lear:* "though Women all aboue: but to the Girdle do the gods inherit, beneath is all the Fiends.

There's hell, there's darkenes, there is the sulphurous pit; burning, scalding, stench, consumption."[52] A similar theme is expressed in sonnet 144, perhaps most aptly, immediately following 143 quoted above

> "Two loves I have, of comfort and despair,/ Which like two spirits do suggest me still;/ The better angel is a man right fair,/ The worser spirit a woman colour'd ill./ To win me soon to hell, my female evil/ Tempteth my better angel from my side,/ And would corrupt my saint to be a devil,/ Wooing his purity with her foul pride ..."

The denigration of the dark lady, and idealisation of his fair friend, is the process of "splitting", projecting all the unacceptable erotic and hostile impulses onto the woman, and all that is noble and virtuous onto the man. It has become commonplace to see Shakespeare's attitude towards his friend as being of a homosexual nature, although the idealised tone of the sonnets would suggest that this was latent rather than actual. This is confirmed by Sonnet 20, in which Shakespeare explicitly repudiates homosexuality: "And for a woman wert thou first created:/ Till nature, as she wrought thee, fell adoting./ And by addition me of thee defeated/ By adding one thing to my purpose nothing./ But since she prick'd thee out for women's pleasure,/ Mine be thy love, and thy love's use their treasure."

In Sonnet 62 Shakespeare explains his love for his young friend as an expression of his own narcissism: "Sin of self- love possesseth all mine eye,/ And all my soul, and all my every part;/ And for this sin there is no remedy,/ It is so grounded in my heart./ Methinks no face so gracious as is mine,/ No shape so true, no truth of such account,/ And for myself mine own worth do define/ As I all other in all worths surmount./ But when my glass shows me myself indeed,/ Beated and chopt with tann'd antiquity,/ Mine own self-love quite contrary I read;/ Self so self-loving were iniquity./ 'Tis thee, my self, that for myself I praise,/ Painting my age with beauty of thy days."

However, in addition to the sonnets, there are a number of the plays, where male characters fall in love with women dressed as men, in which there is a distinct homosexual undertone.[53] The nearest that Shakespeare came to explicit homosexual imagery is in *Venus And Adonis;* at the end of the poem, the encounter between the boar and Adonis is described as follows: "But this foul, grim, and urchin-snouted boar,/ Whose downward eye still looketh for a grave,/ Ne'er saw the beauteous livery that he wore:/ Witness the entertainment that he gave./ If he did see his face, why then I know/ He thought to kiss him, and hath kill'd him so . . . And nuzzling in his flank, the loving swine/ Sheath'd unaware the tusk in his soft groin." Shakespeare's "flight from woman" can be linked, as we saw earlier, to his attitude to marriage. In the play that deals with this theme, *The Comedy Of Errors*, the flight of the husband from his wife is described by Adriana:

> "Whil'st I at home starue for a merrie looke:/ Hath homelie age th' alluring beauty tooke/ From my poor cheeke? then he hath wasted it./ Are my discourses dull? Barren my wit,/ If voluble and sharpe discourse be mar'd,/ Vnkindness blunts it more than marble hard./ Doe their gay vestments his affections baite?/ That's not my fault, he's master of my state./ What ruines in me that can be found,/ By him not ruin'd? Then he is the ground/ Of my defeatures. My decayed faire/ A sunnie looke of his, would soone repaire./ But, too vnruly Deere, he breakes the pale,/ And feedes from home; poore I am but his stale . . . I know his eye doth homage other where,/ Or else, what lets it but he would be here?"[54]

We might say with Bertram, in *All's Well That Ends Well*, that "Warres is no strife/ To the dark house, and the detested wife."[55] And in the light of all the evidence considered in this chapter, perhaps the most apt conclusion about Shakespeare's attitude towards marriage lies in Dromio's comment: "As from a Beare a man would run for life,/ So fly I from her that would be my wife."[56]

CHAPTER 12: BANISHMENT AND EXILE

According to Richard Davies, Shakespeare had been "oft whipt and sometimes imprisoned" for poaching Sir Thomas Lucy's deer. The theme of whipping and banishment is found in a number of the plays, but is most fully explored in *King Lear*. Poor Tom "is whipt from Tything to Tything, and stockt, punish'd, and imprison'd"[1] – a fate which cannot be escaped; as the Fool observes: "they'l have me whipt for speaking true: thou'lt haue me whipt for lying, and sometimes I am whipt for holding my peace."[2] Cornwall punishes Kent by placing him in the stocks, a method of punishment Gloucester considers socially demeaning: "your purpos'd low correction/ Is such as basest and contemned'st wretches/ For pilf'rings and most common trespasses/ Are punish'd with."[3]

In *All's Well That Ends Well*, the Countess playfully teases the clown: "Doe you crie O Lord sir at your whipping, and spare not me? Indeed your O Lord sir, is very sequent to your whipping: you would answere very well to a whipping if you were but bound too't."[4] Later in the play, Lafeu tells Parolles, "you were beaten in *Italy* for picking a kernell out of a Pomgranat"[5], and in the same scene, when the lords deny Helena, he tells her, "And they were sons of mine, I'de haue them whip'd." In *The Winter's Tale*, Autolycus's imaginary robber "was certainely Whipt out of the Court"[6] This, like the previous references, is essentially comic, but in *Anthony And Cleopatra* the tone changes. Anthony has Caesar's messenger whipped:

> "*Anthony* . . . Take hence this Jack, and whip him . . . Whip him Fellowes,/ Till like a Boy you see him crindge his face,/ And whine aloud for mercy . . . Tugge him away: being whipt/ Bring him againe . . . Is he whipt?
> *Enter a Seruant with Thyreus.*
> *Servant* Soundly, my Lord.

Anthony Cried he? and begg'd a Pardon?
Servant He did aske fauour."[7]

A similar tone is adopted by Romeo in describing his punishment: "Shut vp in prison, kept without my foode,/ Whipt and tormented."[8] There are a number of references to whipping for sexual offences: in *All's Well That Ends Well*, there is a hint of Shakespeare's own experience in Parolles description of Dumain: "I know him, a was a Botchers Prentize in *Paris*, from whence he was whipt for getting the Shrieues fool with childe."[9] (According to one tradition, Shakespeare was a butcher's apprentice.) In *Love's Labour Lost*, Costard proposes that "Hector be whipt for *Jaquenetta* that is quicke by him"[10], and in *Midsummers Night Dream*, Lysander proposes that he and Hermia marry at a place remote from Athens, so that "the sharpe Athenian Law/ Cannot pursue vs."[11]

In spite of his belief in a strict social order, Shakespeare displays a profound mistrust of the administration of justice. As Hamlet tells Polonious, "Vse euerie man after his desart, and who shall scape whipping?"[12] And the most famous speech on this subject is of course Lear's bitter diatribe: "See how yond Justice railes vpon yond simple theefe. Hearke, in thine eare: Change places, and handy- dandy, which is the Justice, which is the theefe . . . there thou might'st behold the great image of Authoritie, a Dogg's obey'd in Office. Thou, Rascal Beadle, hold thy bloody hand: why dost thou lash that Whore? Strip thy owne backe, thou hotly lusts to vse her in that kind, for which thou whip'st her."[13] It is difficult not to see in this speech a tinge of Shakespeare's bitterness at his treatment by Sir Thomas Lucy, although obviously it is a great speech on the universal theme of the injustice of the law.

Following punishment, comes banishment and exile. Romeo's reaction to his banishment to Verona, perhaps gives something of what Shakespeare felt at being made to flee Stratford: "Ha, banishment? be mercifull, say death:/ For exile hath more terror in his looke,/ Much more then death: do not say banishment . . . There is no world without *Verona* walles,/ But Purgatorie, Torture, hell it selfe:/ Hence banished, is banisht from the world,/ And worlds exile is death. Then banished,/ Is death, mistearm'd, calling death banished,/ Thou cut'st my head off with a golden Axe,/ And smilest vpon the stroke that murders me."[14]

There is clearly an element of dramatic exaggeration in all this, and it is possible to see exactly the opposite reaction in *Cymbeline*. Belarius and his two adopted sons, Guiderius and Arviragus have been banished to a poor province of Wales, living in the most primitive of circumstances. We have seen earlier how Arviragus champs at being "so long a poor unknown", and this has particular significance because in reality, he is one of the King's lost sons. (This is a familiar theme in Shakespeare: the poor and despised unknown, who in reality is of royal blood.) Like many of Shakespeare's reactions, we can detect strong ambiguity in his attitude to his exile from Stratford: both a banishment and yet at the same time, an escape from the narrow limits of provincial life. But that Shakespeare felt his banishment to be basically a form of exile, is indicated in Sonnet 29:

> "When in disgrace with Fortune and men's eyes,/ I all alone beweep my outcast state,/ And trouble deaf heaven with my bootless cries,/ And look upon myself, and curse my fate,/ Wishing me like to one more rich in hope,/ Featur'd like him, like him with friends possess'd,/ Desiring this man's art, and that man's scope,/ With what I most enjoy contented least;/ Yet in these thoughts myself almost despising,/ Haply I think on thee, and then . . . I scorn to change my state with kings."

The two plays which deal with exile are *King Lear* and *Coriolanus*. Gloucester in his rage with Edgar, gives orders for his capture: "Let him fly farre:/ Not in this Land shall he remain vncaught/ And found; dispatch . . . All Ports Ile barer; the villaine shall not scape . . . besides, his picture I will send farer and neere, that all the kingdome/ May haue due note of him ..."[15] Although highly dramatised, the conditions endured in the flight after banishment, perhaps give us a sense of what Shakespeare endured:

> "Poor naked wretches, where so ere you are/ That bide the pelting of this pittilesse storme,/ . . . Such sheets of Fire, such bursts of horrid Thunder,/ Such groanes of roaring Winde, and Raine, I neuer/ Remember to haue heard. Mans Nature cannot carry/ Th' affliction, nor the feare . . . [so] Tremble thou Wretch/ That hast within thee vndivulged Crimes/ Vnwhipt of justice."[16]

In *Coriolanus*, the bitterness of exile is a central theme. When his wife, mother and son are presented to him, Coriolanus denies all ties: "out affection,/ All bond and priuiledge of Nature breake . . . Ile neuer/ Be such a Gosling to obey instinct: but stand/ As if a man were Author to himself/ & knew no other kin . . . Wife, Mother, Child, I know not . . . Long as my Exile, sweet as my Reuenge!"[17] Final humiliation takes place when Coriolanus enters the foreign city of Antium – perhaps not unlike Shakespeare's arrival in London? – and is refused entry into Aufidius's house:

> "*Coriolanus* A goodly House: The Feast smells well: but I appeare not like a Guest ...

> *1 Servingman* What would you haue Friend? whence are you? Here's no place for you: Pray go to the door ...
> *2 Servingman* Whence are you sir? Ha's the Porter his eyes in his head, that he giues entrance to such Companions? Pray get you out ...
> *3 Servingman* What haue you to do here fellow? Pray you auoid the house.
> *Coriolanus* Let me but stand, I will not hurt your Harth.
> *3 Servingman* What are you?
> *Coriolanus* A Gentleman.
> *3 Servingman* A maru'llous poore one.
> *Coriolanus* True, so I am.
> *3 Servant* Pray you poore Gentleman, take vp some other station: Heere's no place for you . . . Where dwel'st thou?
> *Coriolanus* Vnder the canopy."[18]

There are a number of stories about Shakespeare's arrival in London, but perhaps the most evocative is that told by Robert Shields in the middle of the eighteenth century. Shields claimed that his information originated with William Davenant: "Concerning Shakespear's first appearance in the play-house. When he came to London, he was without money and friends, and being a stranger he knew not to whom to apply, nor by what means to support himself. – At that time coaches not being in use, and as gentlemen were accustomed to ride to the playhouse, Shakespear, driven to the last necessity, went to the playhouse door, and pick'd up a little money by taking care of the gentlemens horses who came to the play; he became eminent even in that profession, and was taken notice of for his diligence and skill in it; he soon had more business than he himself could manage, and at last hired boys under him, who were known by the name of Shakespear's boys: Some of the players accidently conversing with him, found him so acute, and master of so fine a conversation, that struck therewith, they and recommended him to the house."[19]

There are other similar accounts of Shakespeare's employment with horses, written during the middle of the eighteenth century, and although these are too remote in time to be entirely reliable, they confirm what we know from other sources about Shakespeare's poverty and economic destitution during this period. Shields's story has resonance with the account of Coriolanus's reception into the city of Antium quoted above, a similar destitution expressed by Romeo after his banishment from Verona: "Famine is in thy cheekes,/ Need and opression starueth in thy eyes,/ Contempt and beggary hangs vpon thy backe,/ The world is not thy friend, nor the worlds law:/ The world affords no law to make thee rich."[20]

All this is consistent with what we know about the Shakespeare family's economic circumstances during the 1580's. This barren period is reflected in a number of the plays: in *As You Like It*, Orlando complains of his oppression by his brother Oliver: "for my part, he keepes me rustically at home, or (to speak more properly) staies me heere at home vnkept."[21] Likewise, as we have seen, Arviragus laments his narrow and impoverished circumstances – but the seeds of ambition are contained within this narrowness : "Such wind as scatters yongmen throgh ye world,/ To seeke their fortunes farther then at home,/ Where small experience growes."[22] We will consider the fruits of this ambition in the next chapter.

CHAPTER 13: THE RISE OF WILLIAM SHAKESPEARE

In one of the earliest biographical accounts of Shakespeare, John Aubrey described what he had been told at Stratford about Shakespeare's youth: "Mr William Shakespear was borne at Stratford vpon Avon, in the County of Warwick; his father was a Butcher, & I have been told heretofore by some of the neighbours, that when he was a boy he exercised his father's Trade, but when he kill'd a Calfe, he would doe it in a *high style*, & make a Speech. There wast that time another Butcher's son in this Towne, that was held not at all inferior to him in naturall wit, his acquaintance & coetanean, but dyed young."[1]

We have seen that John Shakespeare's main occupation was that of a glover, but he was also a dealer in wool, a money-lender and a trader in a number of other commodities. He controlled about 100 acres of land and probably butchered animals from these and other farms, skinning them to provide materials for his glove-making business. There is some independent confirmation of his trade as a butcher: when his religious testament was discovered at the end of the eighteenth century, a report appeared in the popular press for February 1790: "This testament is no farther remarkable, than in proving that John Shakespear was a Butcher, and that he bequeathed all his acquirements in that profession to his son William."[2] Unfortunately, although now accepted as genuine, this testament was not taken seriously at the time of its discovery; the original manuscript has been lost, and we are unable to check the reliability of this report.

Echoes of Shakespeare's apprenticeship to his father are found in Dowdall's description of his visit to Stratford in about 1693: "the clarke that shew'd me this Church is about 80 yrs old; he says that this *Shakespear* was formerly in this Towne bound apprentice to a butcher; but that he Run from his master to London, and there was Recd Into the playhouse as a serviture."[3] It is likely that the butcher in question was John Shakespeare, and that the flight to London was the result of the deer-poaching incident. As well as mentioning Shakespeare's occupation as a butcher's apprentice, Aubrey also described how "he had been in his younger yeares a Schoolmaster in the Countrey."[4] There has been much speculation about Shakespeare's "lost years", but the only direct information we have comes from the oral tradition, and there is no reason to doubt its veracity on this issue. Shakespeare probably did practice as a country schoolmaster for a while, although he may well have also helped his father on legal matters associated with trading transactions. (His name certainly was linked to his father's in the Lambert dispute.) The most detailed account of these years is that given by Rowe:

> "His Father . . . could give him no better Education than his own Employment. He had bred him, 'tis true, for some time at a Free-School, where 'tis probable he acquir'd that little *Latin* he was Master of: But the narrowness of his Circumstances, and the want of his assistance at Home, forc'd his Father to withdraw him from thence . . . Upon his leaving School, he seems to have given intirely into that way of Living which his Father propos'd to him . . . 'till an Extravagance that he was guilty of, forc'd him both out of his Country and that way of Living which he had taken up."[5]

Therefore it is likely that he was taken away from school at an early age – fourteen? – because of John Shakespeare's difficulties, and that he was apprenticed to his father as a glover/butcher, helping where appropriate with the drafting of bonds and agreements in trading transactions. He also possibly practised as a schoolmaster in the Stratford area – his children were born in Stratford when he was eighteen and twenty-one – perhaps up to the time he left Stratford in his mid-twenties?

But in order to achieve fortune and success, Shakespeare had to renounce the wildness associated with his youth. We have seen how the main dramatic representation of this renunciation, is Hal's rejection of Falstaff, and how this was a metaphor for Shakespeare's rejection of his father's way of life. In *The Merchant Of Venice* and other plays, Shakespeare makes clear his condemnation of usury, in spite of his own father being a money-lender. Shylock embodies all that is morally repugnant and reprehensible, and Shakespeare handles the tension that arises out of this conflict, by creating Jessica's rejection of her father, Shylock: "Alacke, what hainous sinne is it in me/ To be ashamed to be my Fatheres childe/ But though I am a daughter to his blood,/ I am not to his manners."[6]

Although there was a repudiation of the morality of Shylock, there was not a rejection of the ethic of capitalism. Following Max Weber, we may say that Shakespeare renounced the "adventure capitalism" of his father in favour of the more sober, methodical capitalism of the Protestant ethic. He acquired substantial wealth during the 1590's, and carefully invested it in land, property, tithes, as well lending out modest sums at interest. As we have seen, some of this wealth may have come from the gift of one thousand pounds from his patron, the Earl of Southampton, but a substantial proportion undoubtedly accrued through his position as a sharer in both the company and theatre that he worked for. Shakespeare was clearly an astute businessman; and the application for a coat of arms in 1596 was a mark of the success he had achieved in a remarkably short period.

The restoration of the Shakespeare family's fortunes is most clearly delineated in *Cymbeline*. Posthumus reads in gaol of the restoration of Britain's fortunes which echoe Shakespeare's own experience: "When as a Lyons whelpe, shall to himselfe vnknown, without seeking finde, and bee embrac'd by a peece of tender Ayre: And when from a stately Cedar shall be lopt branches, which being dead many yeares, shall after reuive, bee joynted to the old Stocke, and freshly grow, then shall Postumus end his miseries, Britaine be fortunate and flourish in Peace and Plenty."[7]

But there was a negative side to this prosperity. In 1598 Shakespeare became involved in the most controversial of his investments: the hoarding of barley and malt. In order to understand the significance of this, we must appreciate the social changes which were taking place at this time. There had been a significant increase in social polarisation as a result of the demographic and economic changes discussed earlier; in Stratford this had resulted in a sharp rise in the number of poor: a corporation petition stated in 1601 that "our poor are in number seven hundred and odd, young and old" – something like forty per cent of the total population.[8] This increase in poverty was not confined to Stratford: it was a general phenomena throughout England, and perhaps the most vivid illustration of this is the statement made by Phelps-Brown and Hopkins in their study of builders' real wages during the period 1264-1954: "the lowest point we record in seven centuries was in 1597, the year of *Midsummer Night's Dream*."[9]

The problem was compounded in Stratford by the malting industry: barley was used both for malting and for the making of bread, and barley bread was the main food of the poor. As one early seventeenth century observer stated, "Barley is grown into great use of late years . . . and this, in the dear seasons past, the poor found happy benefit, for they were principally relieved and the labourers also fed by the bread made thereof."[10] Barley prices had increased even more significantly than those for wheat (they stood at an index figure of 600 in the 1590's, compared to 499 for wheat[11]), and these were among the reasons why the government passed legislation forbidding the forestalling and hoarding of grain.

There had been a series of very wet seasons in 1594, 1595 and 1596, resulting in scarcity of corn, vaulting prices, and great hardship. In Stratford, on the 4th November 1595, the malsters were bound over not to make malt, and a corn inquiry was carried out the following month. Although a deeply serious matter, there were comic touches about it: the mayor of Stratford, Master Thomas Rogers, bought a cart-load of barley in order to forestall the market, and when reproached for his behaviour, "doth say that he will *justify it*, and he *careth not a turd for them all*." Other leading townsmen were also very active, in particular Shakespeare's friends and associates Abraham Sturley and Richard Quiney, who were listed as "great corn-buyers and buyers of wood and such like".[12] As a result of continuing scarcity, in August 1597, the Privy Council called upon justices of the peace to make an inquisition upon all "engrossers", described as "a nomber of wycked people in condicions more lyke to wolves or cormerants than to naturell men."[13]

As a result of this Privy Council Order, a survey off all those holding grain and corn in Stratford was taken in February 1598. Shakespeare was listed as holding ten quarters of corn in his house at New Place; as Roland Lewis has written about this survey: "In the entire list of one hundred and twenty persons set down, only about a dozen held more 'corne and malte' than Shakespeare . . . In effect . . . [he] took advantage of a prospective rising market in 'corne and malte' and had 'engrossed and forestalled' along with some of his fellow townsmen."[14] The results of this forestalling activity nearly led to bloodshed. On the 24 January 1598, Abraham Sturley wrote a letter to his friend Richard Quiney about the whole affair. Quiney was in London on corporation business, and Sturley, immediately after asking Quiney to approach Shakespeare about investing money in local property, wrote:

> "U shall understande, brother, that our neighbours are growne with the wantes they feele throughe the dearnes of corne, which heare is beionde all other countries that I can heare of deare and over deare, malecontent. Thei

have assembled togeather in a great nomber, and travelld to Sir Tho. Luci on Fridai last to complaine of our malsters; on Sundai to Sir Foulke Gre. and Sir Joh. Conwai. I should have said on Wendsdai to Sir Ed. Grevll first. Theare is a meetinge heare expected tomorrowe. The Lord knoweth to what end it will sorte. Tho. West, returninge from the ij knights of the woodland, came home so full that he said to Mr. Baili that night, he hoped within a weeke to leade some of them in a halter, meaninge the malsters; and I hope, saith Jho. Grannams, if God send mi Lord of Essex downe shortli, to se them hanged on gibbettes att their owne dores."[15]

What the objectors did not realise, was that of the four knights that they protested to, three held stocks of malt in the town on their own behalf. Sir Thomas Lucy was the biggest offender: he held over twelve quarters at Sturley's house (Sturley shared Lucy's puritan sympathies, and at one point worked for him), and sixteen quarters at Richard Dixon's. Sir John Conwayes held over seven quarters "att Rafe Lordes", and Sir Edward Greville held ten quarters, also at Richard Dixon's. Although Sir Fulke Greville did not hold any grain on his own account, his cook, John, held twelve quarters at John Wyllmer's house.[16] It is not suprising that such rebellions had scant chance of success, when the local gentry and magistrates that the protestors looked to for support, were more active in hoarding grain than local townsmen. Also, it explains why the law against forestalling and engrossing was so ineffectual.

The conflicting and contradictory position of the townsmen and local gentry, many of whom were of the puritan persuasion, left them exposed to the charge of hypocrisy. When a dispute over the appointment of the puritan minister, Thomas Wilson, broke out in 1621, his supporters were satirized in the following verse:

"Stratford is a Town that doth make a great show/ But yet is governed but by a few,/ O Jesus Christ of heaven/ I think that they are but seven/ Puritans without doubt/ For you may know them,/ They are so stout,/ They say 'tis no sin, their neighbour's house to take/ But such laws their father the devil did make .../ One of the Chiefest hath read far in Perkin's works,/ The rest are deep dissembling hypocrites."[17]

Shakespeare would have been more than aware of the popular disturbance over the hoarding of grain. Not only had Sturley asked Quiney to contact him in his letter of 24 January where he described the near-riot, but on the 25 October 1598, Quiney wrote to his "Lovinge good ffrend & contreyman Mr Wm. Shackspere."[18] This letter was probably never sent, but Quiney was clearly very friendly with Shakespeare – his son Thomas, married Shakespeare's daughter Judith – and there is no doubt that all these events were reported to Shakespeare by his family and friends on his annual visits to Stratford. In the same way that there were links between John Shakspeare, Henry Rogers, Edward Grant, and Sir Thomas Lucy, there was an equivalent association between William Shakespeare, Richard Quiney, Abraham Sturley and Sir Thomas Lucy. The relationship between Shakespeare and Lucy was a critical one for Shakespeare's personal and social development. The rebel had become the upholder of the very authority which had punished and forced him to flee his home town. Shakespeare adopted the same conservative economic and social position as his former antagonist, and in the process came to share the same capitalistic ethic of acquisition.

Both John and William Shakespeare operated on the margins of the social order: John had risen to prosperity and had virtually achieved gentleman status – fratenizing with local gentry, such as Edward Grant and Sir Thomas Lucy – but then had fallen into destitution and social disgrace. His son had risen from poverty and social stigma into the position of a prosperous gentleman. Shakespeare knew both sides of the social divide, which gave him the experience and knowledge which he exploited so effectively in his plays. But this social experience left its mark on him: his work is shot through with ambiguity and conflict over class issues. In *Julius Caesar*, he comes to an acknowledgement of the effects of social mobility on social perception: "But 'tis a common proofe,/ That Lowlynesse is young Ambitions Ladder,/ Whereto the Climber vpward turnes his Face:/ But when he once attaines the vpmost Round/ He then vnto the Ladder turnes his Backe,/ Lookes in the Clouds, scorning the base degrees/ By which he did ascend."[19]

In *Midsummer Night's Dream*, the artisans are all comic characters, but with a sinister hint of class warfare in the background. We have already noted that the year the play was probably written – 1597 – was a year of great scarcity and hardship, and it is generally recognized that the play makes indirect reference to this. Quince in his reaction to Bottom's lion's roar (in 1, ii) – "you should doe it too terribly, you would fright the Dutchesse and the Ladies, that they would shrike; and that were enough to hang vs all" – is essentially comic, but there is concealed menace in the speech. Likewise later in the play (3, i), Bottom, Snout and Starveling play with the theme of violence, ending with Bottom asking for a prologue which "seeme to say, we will do no harme with our swords". To translate threat into comedy was a socially acceptable way of dealing with the tension arising out of a potentially explosive situation – but it was done at the expense of the artisans, who were seen as suitable for comedy but not serious comment.

It is in the character of Coriolanus, that Shakespeare most embodies the disdain of the successful man for the "base degrees". The play begins with a mutiny over the scarcity of grain, with a population who perceive Coriolanus as "chief enemy to the people". However, although this mutinious population is depicted as fickle, unreliable and open to manipulation by the tribunes, Shakespeare puts speeches into the mouths of citizens, which show considerable sympathy for the plight of ordinary people. Speaking of the rich, the 1st and 2nd Citizens complain:

> "they nere car'd for vs yet. Suffer vs to famish, and their Store-houses cramm'd with Graine: Make Edicts for Vsary, to support Vsurers; repeale daily any wholesome Act established against the rich, and prouide more piercing Statutes daily, to chain vp and restraine the poore . . . We are accounted poore Citizens, the Patricians good: what Authority surfets one, would releeue vs. If they would yeelde vs but the superfluitie while it were wholesome, wee might guess they releeued vs humanely: But they thinke we are too deere, the leanesse that afflicts vs, the object of our misery, is an inuentory to particularize their abundance, our suffering is a gaine to them. Let vs revenge this with our Pikes, ere we become Rakes. For the Gods know, I speake this in hunger for Bread, not in thirst for Reuenge."[20]

This speech and other elements in *Coriolanus* have recently been interpreted by Patterson as referring mainly to various riots which occurred in London, as well as the Midland Revolt of 1607.[21] But of the riots that occurred in London, only two were about food (both in 1595), and they were not about a shortage of grain and basic foodstuffs, but about the price of relative luxuries, fish and butter.[22] Likewise, the Midland Revolt was about the iniquity of enclosures in areas well away from Stratford, and although both series of events may have had an influence on Shakespeare, it is more likely that incidents which directly impinged on his own experience and interest had greater impact. The similarity between the speech quoted above from *Coriolanus* and the sentiments of the Stratford poor reported by Abraham Sturley, are too striking to ignore. Shakespeare had to deal with the tension and ambiguity derived from his situation as a man who had known biting economic adversity, and yet had become a comfortable and successful man of property: in particular, a man who hoarded a large stock of grain during a period of scarcity.

He eventually came down on the side of social order: in *2,Henry VI*, Jack Cade the rebel leader, is depicted as unscrupulous, and ultimately only interested in power and position for himself. There are hints of Orwell's *Animal Farm* in Shakespeare's treatment of this character, and it could be argued that Shakespeare's analysis of rebellion and social order derived ultimately from a realistic understanding of the political-economy of power. But this raises questions beyond the scope of this book, and all we need note here, is the influence of Shakespeare's own position on his political and social perceptions.

In *Timon Of Athens*, Shakespeare reveals the association between personal riot and the breakdown of the social order, a theme which as we have seen, came out of his own experience. Timon in railing against Athens, puts the following curse on the city: "Lust, and Libertie/ Creepe in the Mindes and Marrowes of our youth/ That 'gainst the streame of Vertue they may striue/ And drowne themselues in Riot . . . Piety, and Feare,/ Religion to the Gods, Peace, Justice, Truth,/ Domesticke awe, Night-rest, and Neighbour-hood,/ Instruction, Manners, Mysteries, and Trades,/ Degrees, Obseruances, Customes, and Lawes,/ Decline to your confounding contraries./ And yet Confusion liue."[23] And this prepares the way for Shakespeare's great speech on the breakdown of degree and social order:

> "O, when Degree is shak'd,/ (Which is the Ladder to all high designes)/ The enterprize is sicke. How could Communities,/ Degrees in Schooles, and Brother-hoods in Cities,/ Peacefull Commerce from diuidable shores,/ The primogenitiure, and due of Byrth,/ Prerogatiue of Age, Crownes, Scepters, Lawrels,/ (But by Degree) stand in Authentique place?/ Take but Degree away, vn-tune that string,/ And hearke what Discord followes: each thing meetes/ In meere oppugnancie. The bounded Waters/ Should lift their bosomes higher then the Shores,/ And make a soppe of all this solid Globe:/ Strength should be Lord of imbecility,/ And the rude sonne should strike his Father dead:/ Force should be right, or rather, right and wrong,/ (Between whose endlesse jarre, Justice recides)/ Should loose her names, and so should Justice too./ Then euerything includes it selfe in Power,/ Power into Will, Will into Appetite,/ And Appetite (an vniuersall Wolfe,/ So doubly seconded with Will, and Power)/ Must make perforce an vniuersall prey,/ And last, eate up himselfe."[24]

Here Shakespeare surpasses himself with the brilliance of his imagery and language, surely an unrivalled statement of the conservative case for social and political order. In creating this statement however, he sublimated the tensions and ambiguities of his own personal situation. The speech resonates with aggression and rage, but this in no way detracts from the scale of his achievement. All thinkers who have addressed the problem of human nature and its social containment have had to deal with the issue of aggression and violence, and Shakespeare's individual experience in no way limits the universal applicability of this speech. However, underneath this conservative apotheosis, the personal and social tensions remained – and this is the subject of our final and concluding chapter.

CHAPTER 14: THE END OF EXILE

The play in which Shakespeare explored most directly the tensions arising out of violence was *Hamlet*. Ernest Jones and others have analysed the play's psychological dimensions, and it has been examined from a number of other perspectives, all of which have brought out its great richness and complexity. What has yet to be undertaken, is a sociological analysis of the context of the play, something which will enable us to examine certain key strands in Shakespeare's own biography. Although there are a number of themes in the play, the interplay between murder and suicide is one of its central ones. *Hamlet* has mainly been interpreted in terms of the motivations of individual characters, but Shakespeare expressed much more than the personal in the play. It reflected a general cultural shift which was taking place at the time: a historical decline in the overall level of overt violence which occurred in England from about the thirteenth century onwards.[1]

The reasons for this diminishing violence are complex: one factor may have been the growth of literacy, particulary in urban areas, but another factor has been noted by J. B. Given in his study of homicide in thirteenth century England. He found that the murder rate was lower in large towns, such as London, than in rural areas, and has argued that this can partly be explained by the culture of individualism which had developed in the towns. Much homicide was communal in nature – a residue of the blood feud – and paradoxically, the relative social isolation of the townsman, led to a reduction in the level of violence.[2] But a decrease in homicide was associated with a growth in suicide. Durkheim showed in his classic study of suicide, that the individualism associated with town life, frequently engendered what he termed "egoistic" suicide: suicide resulting from excessive self- preoccupation, over-intellectualisation, and an inability to act[3]: all characteristics associated with Hamlet, and also shown in some of Shakespeare's sonnets, particularly sonnet 62.

The atmosphere and culture of late sixteenth century London was in certain respects unique: all the evidence is that London was a much more literate and less violent place than the country at large. Sharpe in his study of crime in early modern England noted from an analysis of indictments for felony during 1550-1625, that the metropolitan county of Middlesex showed "differences from those derived from rural areas." Of all those indicted for felonies, only five per cent of those in Middlesex were for homicide and infanticide, whereas the figure in more rural counties were mainly in the range of nine to sixteen per cent.[4] Although there were a number of popular disorders in late sixteenth century London – there were at least ninety-six outbreaks in London between 1517 and 1640, of which thirty-five took place between 1581 and 1602[5] – most of these were not of a violent nature. John Graunt in his study of the London bills of mortality, provided a series of figures confirming London's relatively non-violent reputation. During the eight-year period 1629-36, twenty-nine people were murdered, compared fifty-five people committing suicide, giving a homicide rate of 1.51 per 100,000 and a suicide rate of 2.86.[6] The homicide rate was very low compared to that for the rest of the country: in thirteenth century England it was in the range of 9.0 to 47.0 per 100,000, while other research indicates a rate for the country as a whole during the sixteenth and seventeenth century period of 5.0 – 18.0 per 100,000.[7] The low homicide figure for London persisted through the seventeenth and into the eighteenth century, and the rate was very similar to that for England today. That this low murder rate was genuine was confirmed by Graunt, who was born in London, and lived in the city through the period in question. In attempting to explain the very small number of murders in London, Graunt wrote in 1662:

> "My next Observation is; That but few are *Murthered*, viz. not above 86 of the 22950 which have died of other diseases [in the period 1629-58], and casualities; whereas in *Paris* few might scape without their *Tragedie*. The Reasons of this we conceive to be *Two: One is the Government*, and *Guard* of the City by *Citizens* themselves . . . And the other is, The natural, and customary abhorrance of that inhumane *Crime*, and all *Bloodshed* by most *Englishmen:* for all that are executed, few are for *Murther* . . . In brief, when any dead Body is found in *England*, no *Algebraist*, or *Uncipherer* of Letters, can use more subtile, and varitie of conjectures to finde out the Demonstration, or Cipher; then every common unconcerned person doth to finde out the Murtherers, and that for ever, untill it be done."[8]

Graunt's belief in the "customary abhorrence" against "all bloodshed" may have been typical of most Londoners, but it was not characteristic of the English population as a whole. His explanations for this very low rate in London are not very convincing. No doubt having the city policed by its own citizens helped reduce the frequency of murder to some extent, but perhaps more important was the relative anonymity of a large city like London – social distance minimizes emotional contact and the basis of dispute. (London's population doubled in the last two decades of the sixteenth century, and the majority of its population were immigrants – and therefore, in the main, strangers to each other.) Additionally, Londoners were a very well-educated population compared to the country generally; whereas 72 per cent of the latter were unable to sign the Protestation Oath of 1642, "the two London parishes for which usable returns survive have the remarkably low rate of 28 per cent."[9] The inhibiting effect of education and rational thought – Hamlet's "pale cast of thought" – operated in London's more literate culture. (This was re-inforced by the puritanism of the city corporation – there being a general association between literacy and the spread of puritanism.) The "abhorrence" against "all bloodshed" was of course a matter of degree: the bear and bull-baitings that took place near the Globe Theatre in Southwark, are reminders that London was not an entirely unviolent city.

In this context, Ernest Jones's reference to Hamlet as the first modern man is very apt: Hamlet, whose "hue of resolution/ Is sicklied o'er with the pale cast of thought", embodies the irreconcilable conflict between the aggressive and the rational. Aggression inhibited by rational restraint is invariably internalised, and turned against the self: it is partly for this reason that most modern societies have relatively low homicide but high suicide rates.[10] Aggression directed inwards leads to self-denigration, resulting in melancholy and depression, culminating in *extremis* in suicide – all feelings and reactions experienced by Hamlet. Shakespeare himself expressed similar feelings of self-depreciation and personal unworthiness in some of the sonnets.

However, we must not exaggerate the decline in overt violence during Shakespeare's period; for example, Gough recorded ten murders in and around the village of Myddle in Shropshire for the seventeenth century. Although not all the murders took place in the village itself, it only had a population of about six hundred people, and therefore was a very violent place by modern standards. We do not have enough information on the sociological history of Stratford, to know whether it was as violent as this

Shropshire village, although on an anecodotal level, this appears to have been the case. For example, Shakespeare had bought New Place in 1597, and the two previous owners, William Bott and William Underhill, were both involved in murders: Bott poisoned his own daughter, and Underhill in turn was poisoned by his eldest son. (It is possible that these incidents influenced Shakespeare's choice of the method of murder for King Hamlet.) Likewise, Shakespeare's friend and associate, Richard Quiney, died in 1602 after having been wounded in a drunken brawl with some of Sir Edward Greville's men.[11] We have already seen how frequent were the fights between townsmen in Stratford, and in order to attempt to control physical violence, the corporation on more than one occasion banned single men from carrying weapons in the town.

Thus Shakespeare's move from Stratford to London was cultural as well as geographical. The movement between the two worlds is echoed in the description of Hal's transformation in *Henry V:* "His Houres fill'd vp with Ryots, Banquets, Sports;/ And neuer noted in him in any studie,/ Any retyrement, and sequestration . . . Consideration like an Angell came/ And whipt th'offending *Adam* out of him . . . Neuer was such a sodaine Scholler made:/ Neuer came Reformation in a Flood ..." All that we know about Shakespeare suggests that he underwent a similar transformation; having spent his youth in "wild riot", he became in his maturity, a man of reserved and private habits. Aubrey in the material he collected for his *Brief Lives* (probably from the actor Beeston), described Shakespeare's social life: "he was not a company keeper [-] lived in Shoreditch, wouldnt be debauched, & if invited to [-] writ; he was in paine."[12]

The evidence from the Belott-Mountjoy suit confirms this picture of a private and modest life-style: Shakespeare lodged with the Mountjoys, who were a Huguenot family, and helped arrange the marriage between Mountjoy's daughter and his apprentice Bellott. Shakespeare's relative isolation is suggested by the tone and substance of a number of the sonnets – "I all alone beweep my outcast state" – and this was an expression of the sense of exile discussed earlier. This however must be qualified by the anecdotes which describe Shakespeare enjoying the company of friends. The sonnets suggest that most of his friendships were intensely private, although with fellow writers such as Jonson and Drayton, he is reported to have spent time in drinking and social companionship, particularly in later life.[13]

It is perhaps more apt to see Shakespeare living in a transitional period, when the "blood and roses" of the medieval world were beginning to give way to the more constrained and literate culture of town life. Nevertheless, Shakespeare's place of origin, Stratford, was in many respects similar to Gough's rural world – a world which had not yet been "civilised", a world of raw physical and social intensities, which modern man would find very frightening. Shakespeare in fleeing from Stratford, left behind this raw, physical world, with its passionate acting out of impulse and feeling, and entered Freud's "civilization and its discontents". This new civilized world was one of culture and great artistic creativity, but it carried with it all the personal tensions and neuroses so painstakingly depicted by Freud.

Shakespeare's attempt to resolve these tensions culminated in *The Tempest*. We have seen that Shakespeare partially achieved this by "splitting" his own biographical presence into the characters of Prospero and Caliban. Prospero's power is used in the service of moral revenge against all those who have usurped his rightful position, and have been responsible for his exile. This allowed Shakespeare to finally sublimate his own aggression into a morally acceptable position – although at the cost of having created Caliban, a metaphor for alienated man. *The Tempest* announces the end of exile: "I'le breake my staffe,/ Bury it certaine fadomes in the earth,/ And deeper than did euer Plummet sound/ Ile drowne my booke."[14] This renunciation of Prospero's power – based on his command of the written word – signals Shakespeare's retirement from the stage and his return to his home town, Stratford.

★ ★ ★

Before returning to Stratford, Shakespeare had to bring about a psychological reconciliation with his wife, and this was achieved in *The Winter's Tale*. Leontes, having effectively killed his wife Hermione, is finally forgiven: "Sir, you haue done enough, and haue perform'd/ A Saint-like Sorrow:/ No fault could you make,/ Which you haue not redeem'd; indeed pay'd downe/ More penitence then done trespass: At the last/ Doe as the Heauens have done; forget your euil,/ With them, forgiue your selfe."[15] In the final extraordinary scene in the play, Hermione, who has been pretending to be a statue for twenty years, comes to life, and Shakespeare describes the reconciliation between her and Leontes through Paulina's speech as follows:

> "Musick; awake her: Strike:/ 'Tis time: descend: be Stone no more: approach:/ Strike all that looke vpon with meruaile: Come:/ Ile fill your Graue vp: stirre: nay, come away:/ Bequeath to Death your numnesse: (for from him/ Deare Life redeemes you) you perceiue she stirres:/ Start not: her Actions shall be holy, as/ You heare my Spell is lawfull: doe not shun her,/ Vntil you see her dye againe; for then You kill her double: Nay, present your Hand:/ When she was young, you woo'd her: now, in age,/ Is she become the Suitor?"[16]

There is a note of ambiguity in this reconciliation: although Hermione is brought back to life, there is a hint of reluctance on Leontes's part, as he hesitates to take her hand – perhaps an ambiguity reflected in the famous "second-best bed" that Shakespeare left to his wife? On retirement, Shakespeare went back to live in Stratford, and so returned to live with his wife after a twenty-year-or-so absence. Rowe described his retirement as follows:

> "The latter Part of his Life was spent, as all Men of good Sense will wish theirs to be, in Ease, Retirement, and the Conversation of his Friends. He had the good Fortune to gather an Estate equal to his Occasion, and, in that, to his Wish; and is said to have spent some Years before his Death at his native *Stratford*. His pleasurable Wit, and good Nature, engag'd him in the Acquaintance, and entitled him to the Friendship of the Gentlemen of the Neighbourhood. Amongst them, it is a Story almost still remember'd in that Country, that he had a particular Intimacy with Mr *Combe*, an old Gentleman noted there-abouts for his Wealth and Usury: It happen'd, that in a pleasant Conversation amongst their common Friends, Mr *Combe* told *Shakespear* in a laughing manner, that he fancy'd, hed intended to write his Epitath, if he happen'd to out-live him; and since he could not know what might be said of him when he was dead, he desir'd it might be done immediately: Upon which *Shakespear* gave him these four verses. *Ten in the Hundred lies here ingrav'd,/ 'Tis a Hundred to Ten, his Soul is not sav'd:/ If any Man ask, Who lies in this Tomb?/ Oh! ho! quoth the Devil, 'tis my* John-a-Combe. But the Sharpness of the Satyr is said to have stung the Man so severely, that he never forgave it."[17]

Rowe's account indicates that Shakespeare had achieved in retirement a form of resolution to the various personal and social tensions which had bedevilled his earlier life. His sociability and enjoyment of the company of good friends, hints at a life of contentment, but even in this, there is a note of ambiguity: the satire on Coombe, who had puritan leanings, is a reminder of the ambivalence of Shakespeare's relationship with his father, who like Coombe, had been a money- lender. Also, within the good companionship and enjoyable sociability, there was a hint of an old problem, that seems never to have entirely disappeared. There are a number of stories within the traditional *corpus*, that mention Shakespeare's drinking bouts in Stratford and surrounding villages. The strongest and most important is that given by John Ward, who was vicar of Stratford during the years 1662-81. Ward kept note-books and some time during 1661-63, made the following note about Shakespeare's death: "Shakespear, Drayton, and Ben Jhonson, had a merry meeting, and it seems drank too hard, for Shakespear died of a feavour there contracted . . ."[18]

How ironic, given his father's history, that Shakespeare is reported to have died from excessive drinking. The play in which Shakespeare's own attitude to drink is explored most directly is *The Tempest*. Caliban is the repository of all that is dark and malignant: he attempts to rape Miranda, is treacherous, and plans to murder Prospero. His malignacy is fed by addiction to drink, to which he is introduced by Stephano and Trinculo. He comes to worship Stephano, a drunken butler, as a result of drinking from "a butt of sack"; he offers to render Stephano all the services that he has been forced to give to Prospero. As Trinculo says of him: "A most rediculous Monster, to make a wonder of a poore drunkard."[19] And at the end of the play, Caliban comes to renounce Stephano, in the way that Hal rejects Falstaff: "what a thrice-double Asse/ Was I to take this drunkard for a god?/ And worship this dull foole?"[20]

As we have seen, Caliban is Prospero's "shadow" – "this thing of darkness I/ Acknowledge mine" – and as Prospero is widely recognized as a character with strong autobiographical associations, Caliban can be seen as a metaphor for Shakespeare's own "dark side". The power that Prospero has over Caliban resides in his books: "Remember/ First to possesse his Bookes; for without them/ Hee's but a Sot, as I am"[21] – a remarkable confirmation of the linkage between Prospero and Caliban, and the hidden world of alcoholism. It is as if there is a war between the world of the "book" and that of the "bottle": both having an almost magical power over men's lives, and Caliban pleads for Stephano to remove Trinculo's bottle, in the same way that he demands the seizure of Prospero's books. We see here a re-surfacing of the issue of wildness and its containment by rationality: a containment which was always very fragile, and which was constantly under threat of breakdown through alcoholic drink. But perhaps this ambiguity and ambivalence is an inevitable condition of "civilized life", and a point has now been reached where we must sum up and draw conclusions for our understanding of Shakespeare's biography.

★ ★ ★

John Shakespeare stands at the centre of this book, and he is the key figure in the life and writings of his son William. Not only did he have a profound effect through his larger-than-life personality – his wit, his sophistication and gargantuan appetite for life – but created the conditions responsible for Shakespeare's exile from his home and family. John Shakespeare as Falstaff embodied physicality, spontaneity, and all the qualities that Freud described in the concept of the "id". He also displayed the cunning and intellectual virtuosity of the cosmopolitan trader – Freud's "ego" – and we can see in John Shakespeare the two worlds which were to shape Shakespeare's life: the raw and violent physicality of Stratford, and the intellectual and cultural world of London. Running through these two worlds was a common thread: an addiction to drink, with all that it represented – not only the sociability of the inns of Stratford, London and elsewhere, but the eventual decline into poverty and social humiliation.

For Shakespeare, this licentiousness was mirrored by the wildness of his own youth: the poaching of deer and rabbits, his rebelliousness against authority, and the youthful enjoyment of sexual pleasure, culminating in Anne Hathaway's pregnancy and early marriage. There was a direct parallel between John Shakespeare's addiction to drink, and his son's love of sport and pleasure. Falstaff as a figure comes to embody both these strands, and his rejection represents not only a turning away from John Shakespeare and his way of life, but a repudiation of Shakespeare's own wildness. In the way that John Shakespeare had undergone "gravity's revolt to wantoness", Shakespeare experienced the reverse: from "Ryots, Banquets, Sports" to a "sodaine Scholler made". The linking of opposites is a commonplace, with a psychological affinity between the puritan and the drunkard – expressed so well by Caliban in his description of Prospero: for without his books, "Hee's but a Sot, as I am."

Shakespeare's flight to London was the direct result of his poaching activities, but was associated with his abandonment of his wife in Stratford. In the process, he became a private man: the outcast individual, diligently pursuing his calling, and in many ways his new life was characterized by Weber's protestant ethic: resulting in a methodical pursuit of economic success and wealth. Behind this quest for prosperity lay the shadow of social humiliation deriving from his father's poverty and debt – felt all the more keenly because of the prosperity and success which had preceeded it. In this respect, Shakespeare's life is yet a further example of Edmund Wilson's "wound and the bow": the wound of personal trauma fuelling the drive for artistic success. For Shakespeare, much of this ambition was strictly economic: the restoration of family fortunes became a key imperative, and as Pope observed, much of the motivation for writing the plays was commercial rather than aesthetic. (Thus the fact that only about half the plays were published in Shakespeare's lifetime – their non-publication representing a commercial advantage in an age when a monopoly of material for stage production was more important than revenue from the sale of books.)

But beyond the realm of the economic, Shakespeare's work is an affirmative expression of "the uses of adversity". Out of the misfortunes of his exiled state, came the striving to overcome his afflicted condition. There is something of a quest for superiority to compensate for feelings of inferiority in this – as described by Adler – but perhaps Nietchze's "will to power" is a more appropriate metaphor, particularly as represented in the figure of Coriolanus. The result of this striving was a steady accumulation of capital and the eventual restoration of family fortunes. From this accumulation, came the portly figure – bourgeois, successful and comfortable – depicted in the bust placed in Stratford church. Shakespeare embraced capitalism just as enthusiastically as his father, although with him it was less adventure capitalism, and more the methodical variety associated with the protestant ethic. (It is perhaps no accident that he had lodged with a Huguenot family, was friendly with the puritan Coombe family at the end of his life, and had a son-in-law and daughter with puritan leanings.)

Beyond this comfortable puritanism, lay the profound consciousness of "modern man": an existential awareness of the ultimate aloneness of the individual, with a resulting sense of exile. But even here, John Shakespeare played a pivotal role: his death ushered in the "dark period", in which Shakespeare wrote all the great tragedies, with a series of tragically afflicted heroes. Yet Shakespeare was able to transcend the exile and alienation – "my outcast state" – through a self-affirmation, which used the adversities and difficulties of his youth to create the successes of his later, mature life. Shakespeare's genius was to translate the culture of his early life – characterized by all its intensities – into the new literacy associated with his London experience, using his "natural wit" to create the great comedies, histories and tragedies. In this respect, we can say that he followed Freud's dictum: "where id was, ego shall be" – with all the ambiguities and tensions that inevitably result. In the process, he sublimated his own inner torments and conflicts, to achieve artistic and economic success, returning to Stratford and bringing about an end to exile. It is perhaps therefore appropriate, to conclude with a quote from Shakespeare, which epitomises the fundamental self-affirmation which lies at the centre of his life and work:

> "Sweet are the uses of adversity, which like a toad, ugly and venemous, wears yet a precious jewel in his head. And this our life, exempt from public haunt, finds tongues in trees, books in the running brooks, sermons in stones, and good in everything."[22]

FOOTNOTES

CHAPTER 1: INTRODUCTION

1 E.K.Chambers, *William Shakespeare: A Study Of Facts And Problems*, Vol.2 (1930), p.247
2 Richard Gough, *The History Of Myddle* (Ed. P.E.Razzell, Caliban Books, 1979)

CHAPTER 2: THE RISE OF JOHN SHAKESPEARE

1 F.E.Halliday, *A Shakespeare Companion* (1964), pp 441, 442
2 D.L.Thomas and N.E.Evans, "John Shakespeare In The Exchequer", *Shakespeare Quarterly*, Vol. 35 (1984), p.318
3 Sidney Lee, *Stratford-on-Avon* (1890), p.110
4 *The Victoria County History Of Warwickshire*, Vol. 3 (1945), p.236
5 *Ibid*, p.236
6 *Ibid*, p.240
7 *Ibid*
8 Lee, *op.cit.*, p.109
9 E.A.Wrigley & R.S.Schofield, *The Population History Of England* (1980), p.208
10 B.R.Mitchell and P.Deane, *Abstract Of British Historical Statistics* (1971), pp 484-486
11 Joan Thirsk (Ed), *The Agrarian History Of England And Wales, Vol. 4: 1500-1640* (1967), pp 857, 858; E.H.Phelps-Brown and Sheila V.Hopkins, "Seven Centuries Of The Prices Of Consumables,

Compared With Builders' Wage Rates" in E.M.Carus-Wilson (Ed), *Essays In Economic History*, Vol. 2 (1962), pp 193-195

12 Thirsk, *op.cit.*,p.861

13 E.Kerridge, *The Agricultural Revolution* (1967); J.A.Sharpe, *Early Modern England : A Social History 1550-1760* (1987), p.134

14 Victor Skipp, *Crisis And Development: An Ecological Case Study Of The Forest Of Arden, 1570-1674* (1978), pp 13, 47

15 *Ibid*, pp 68, 71

16 *Ibid*, p.62

17 *Ibid*, p.70

18 *Ibid*, p.70

19 *Ibid*, p.71

20 *Ibid*, p.56

21 *Ibid*, pp 70, 72

22 Robert Finlay, *Population And Metropolis: The Demography Of London* (1981), pp 6, 51

23 J.M.Martin, *Population And Mortality In Tudor And Stuart Stratford* (1972) (Manuscript thesis in the Warwickshire County Record Office), p.45

24 *The Registers Of Stratford-On-Avon*, Ed. Richard Savage (Parish Register Society, 1897-1905)

25 *Ibid;* Edgar Fripp, *Shakespeare: Man And Artist*, Vol.1 (1938), p.40; Vol.2 (1938), pp 491, 492

26 Finlay, *op.cit.*, p.9

27 See Edgar Fripp, *Master Richard Quyney* (1924), p.103; B.Rowland Lewis, *The Shakespeare Documents*, Vol.1 (1940), pp 281, 285

28 Fripp, *Quyney op.cit.*, p.104

29 I have used the Phelps-Brown & Hopkins price index for the period 1570-79 as the base figure, and inflated it using their series up to 1954. See Phelps-Brown & Hopkins, pp 193-195. For the post-1954 period I have used *Department of Employment, Retail Price Indices 1914-1986* (HMSO, 1987), p.1, and the *Central Statistics Office, Annual Abstract of Statistics* (1990), p.322, and *Employment Gazette, February 1990*, p.55. The inflation ratio of 140 is a conservative one, in particular with respect to house prices, which are not included in the ratio. House prices rose much more significantly than other prices: for example, Shakespeare appears to have paid about £60 for New Place in 1597; an equivalent house today would be worth at least £300,000, giving an inflation ratio of 500.

30 Skipp, *op.cit.*, p.9
31 Lewis, *op.cit.*, pp 149-152
32 *Ibid*, p.130
33 *Ibid*, p.53
34 *Ibid*, p.64
35 Thirsk, *op.cit.*, p.857
36 Richard Savage and Edgar Fripp (Eds), *Minutes And Accounts Of The Corporation Of Stratford-Upon-Avon And Other Records, Vol.1: 1553-1566* (Dugdale Society, 1921), pp 47,48
37 *Ibid*
38 Lewis, *op.cit.*, p.63
39 Thomas & Evans, *op.cit.*. The following discussion is based on this article.
40 Lewis, *op.cit.*,p.68
41 *Ibid*, p.64
42 *Ibid*

CHAPTER 3: JOHN SHAKESPEARE'S CULTURAL WORLD

1 Lewis, *op.cit.*, p.139
2 Alan Everitt, "The Marketing of Agricultural Produce", in Joan Thirsk, *op.cit.*, pp 543-563. The discussion of free individual trading relies heavily on Everitt's work.
3 *Ibid*, p.543
4 Peter J.Bowden, *The Wool Trade In Tudor And Stuart England* (1962), p.82
5 *Ibid*
6 *Ibid*, p.91
7 *Ibid*, p.96
8 *Ibid*, p.101
9 Everitt, *op.cit.*, p.557
10 *Ibid*, pp 558, 559
11 *Ibid*, p.561
12 *Ibid*, p.563
13 *Ibid*
14 S.Schoenbaum, *William Shakespeare: A Compact Documentary Life* (1987), p.37

15 Lewis, *op.cit.*, p.230
16 Halliday, *op.cit.*, pp 399, 400
17 Lewis, *op.cit.*, p.54
18 See Savage & Fripp, *op.cit.*, Vol.1 (1921) & Vol.2 (1924)
19 *Ibid*, Vol.2 (1924)
20 *Ibid*, p.112
21 *Ibid*, Vol.3 (1926), p.10
22 *Ibid*, pp 24, 31
23 Fripp, *Shakespeare Man And Artist*, Vol.1, p.76
24 Savage & Fripp, *op.cit.*, Vol.3, p.170
25 M.Eccles, *Shakespeare In Warwickshire* (1961), p.27
26 Chambers, *William Shakespeare*, Vol.2, p.20
27 Savage & Fripp, *op.cit.*, Vol.2, p.xlv
28 See for example *Ibid*, Vol.3, p.10
29 *Ibid*, Vol.1, pp 128, 138, 139
30 H.Mutschmann and K.Wentersdorf, *Shakespeare And Catholicism* (1952), p.39
31 *Ibid*, p.42
32 Savage & Fripp, *op.cit.*, Vol.1, p.xxxix
33 *Victoria County History Of Warwickshire*, Vol.3 (1945), p.281
34 Savage & Fripp, *op.cit.*, Vol.2, p.92
35 *Ibid*, Vol.4 (1929), p.13
36 See *Ibid*, Vols. 1-4
37 Fripp, *Master Richard Quyney*, pp 47, 48
38 See Savage & Fripp, *op.cit.*, Vols. 1-4 for many references
39 Fripp, *Shakespeare Man And Artist*, Vol.1, p.156
40 *Ibid*, p.151
41 *Ibid*, p.78
42 Mutschmann & Wentersdorf, *op.cit.*, p.44
43 *Ibid*, p.46
44 For a discussion of this, see Schoenbaum, *op.cit.*, pp 45-53
45 Eccles, *op.cit.*, pp 33, 34
46 *Ibid*,, p.33
47 Savage & Fripp, *op.cit.*, Vol.4, pp 57-60
48 Eccles, *op.cit.*, p.33
49 *Ibid*,, p.33

CHAPTER 4: THE SHAKESPEARE/LAMBERT DISPUTE

1 Lewis, *op.cit.*, p.135
2 *Ibid*, p.113
3 *Ibid*, pp 132, 133
4 *Ibid*, p.133
5 *Ibid*, pp 138, 139
6 "Shakespeare In The Public record Office", *Public Record Office Handbook*, No.5 (1964), p.6
7 Lewis, *op.cit.*, pp 140, 141
8 *Ibid*, pp 142, 143
9 *Ibid*, p.144
10 Eccles, *op.cit.*, p.29
11 Schoenbaum, *op.cit.*, p.39
12 Halliday, *op.cit.*, p.443
13 Lewis, *op.cit.*, p.145
14 *Ibid*, pp 141, 143
15 Schoenbaum, *op.cit.*, pp 40, 41
16 Eccles, *op.cit.*, p.31
17 Schoenbaum, *op.cit.*, pp 15, 16
18 See Savage & Fripp, *op.cit.*, Vols 1-4
19 See P.E.Razzell, "Introduction" in Richard Gough, *History Of Myddle* (Caliban Books, 1979)

CHAPTER 5: JOHN SHAKESPEARE AS FALSTAFF

1 Savage & Fripp, *op.cit.*, Vol.4, p.161
2 Schoenbaum, *op.cit.*, p.332
3 J.O.Halliwell-Phillips, *The Life Of William Shakespeare* (1848), p.127
4 Eccles, *op.cit.*, p.34
5 *Ibid*
6 Chambers, *op.cit.*, p.247. The only known Sir John Mennis alive in this period was far too young (he was born in 1599) to have met Shakespeare's father, who died in 1601. However, as Eccles points out,"Mennis, who collected poems and anecdotes, may have borrowed the story from an earlier visitor to Stratford." Eccles, *op.cit.*, p.71. As Mennis was a friend of Sir William D'Avenant, reputed

illegitimate son of Shakespeare, it is possible that D'Avenant was the source. The authenticity of the story is indicated by Plume/Mennis's knowledge of John Shakespeare's occupation as a glover – something no other contemporary writer was aware of.

7 E.K.Chambers, *Sources For A Biography of Shakespeare* (1946), p.10; Lewis, *op.cit.*, p.8

8 W.H.Auden, "The Prince's Dog" in G.K.Hunter (Ed),*Shakespeare Henry IV Parts 1 and 2* (1970), pp 187, 188

9 Chambers, *William Shakespeare*, Vol.2, p.266. The Reference to £1,000 also occurs in *Much Ado About Nothing*, 1, i and 3, iv

10 R.B.Wheeler, *History And Antiquities of Stratford-Upon-Avon* (1806), p.73

11 Chambers, *op.cit.*, p.20. £500 was the sum that Shallow asked back from Falstaff when he discovered that Falstaff was to be banished.

12 *2, Henry IV*, 733-735,in *The First Folio Of Shakespeare* (Norton Facsimile Edition, edited by Charlton Hinman, 1968). All references to Shakespeare's plays will be to this Folio edition, using the line numbering system, unless otherwise stated. All other references to Shakespeare's sonnets and poems will be from Peter Alexander, *William Shakespeare: The Complete Works* (1951).

13 Chambers, *op.cit.*, pp 19, 21

14 *Ibid*, pp 26, 28-32; Eccles, *op.cit.*, p.17

15 Schoenbaum, *op.cit.*, p.229

16 The reference to Jonson's visit to Stratford was for the year of Shakespeare's death, but it is possible that he had made earlier visits. According to John Ward, Vicar of Stratford in 1662-81, "Shakspear, Drayton, and Ben Jhonson, had a merry meeting, and itt seems drank too hard, for Shakespear died of a feavour there contracted." See Halliday, *op.cit.*, p.520

17 Ronald McKerrow (Ed), *The Works Of Thomas Nashe*, Vol.1 (1966), p.171

18 *1,Henry IV*, 1183

19 *2,Henry,IV*, 2353-2361

20 *Henry V*, 2267-2270

21 *Ibid*, 2627-2633

22 *Ibid*, 2934-2947

23 *2,Henry,IV*, 3231-3234 & 3247-3266

24 *Henry V*, 587

25 Eccles, *op.cit.*, p.35

CHAPTER 6: THE FALL OF JOHN SHAKESPEARE

1 Fripp, *Shakespeare Man & Artist*, p.151
2 *Hamlet* (Quarto Edition, 1604), 1, iv
3 Harold Jenkins (Ed.), *Hamlet* (The Arden Edition, 1982), p. 448
4 McKerrow, *op.cit.*, p.205
5 *Othello*, 1188-1197
6 *The Rape Of Lucrece*
7 *Timon Of Athens*, 832-837
8 *Ibid*, 657-659
9 Everitt, *op.cit.*, pp 567, 568
10 Lewis, *op.cit.*, p.241
11 Everitt, *op.cit.*, p.568
12 Quoted in Max Weber, *The Protestant Ethic And The Spirit Of Capitalism* (1930), p.175
13 Everitt, *op.cit.*, p.572
14 Savage and Fripp, *op.cit.*, Vol.1, pp xxi, xxii
15 *Ibid*, Vol.4, p.165
16 Fripp, *Master Richard Quyney*, p.133
17 Halliwell-Phillips, *Outlines*, Vol.1, p.142

CHAPTER 7: THE DEATH OF JOHN SHAKESPEARE AND THE WRITING OF HAMLET

1 Halliday, *op.cit.*, p.204
2 Jenkins, *op.cit.*, pp 573, 574
3 *Ibid*, p.4
4 L.Kirschbaum, "The Date Of Shakespeare's *Hamlet*", *Studies In Philology*, Vol.34 (1937)
5 *Hamlet*, 2, ii
6 See Fredson Bowers, *Introductions, Notes And Commentaries To Texts In 'The Dramatic Works Of Thomas Dekker'*, Vol.1 (1980), pp 179-196 for this and other information on the dispute.
7 C.H.Heford and Percy Simpson, *Ben Jonson*, Vol.4 (1980), p.203
8 *Ibid*, p.251
9 *Ibid*, p.255
10 *Ibid*, pp 255, 256

11 *Ibid*, pp 320, 321
12 Bowers, *op.cit.*, p.180
13 *Ibid*, p.181, fn 5
14 Quoted in *Ibid*, p.196
15 Halliday, *op.cit.*, p.157
16 *Hamlet* (First Quarto, 1603), Scene vii
17 *Hamlet*, 780-789
18 *Hamlet*, 250-288
19 *Hamlet*, 1342-1346
20 *Hamlet*, 2917-2919 & 2941-2948
21 *Hamlet* (Second Quarto, 1604), 5, i. There are echoes of this speech in *Titus Andronicus:* "*Lucius:* Come hither, boy; come, come, and learn of us/ To melt in showers. Thy grandsire lov'd thee well;/ Many a time he danc'd thee on his knee,/ Sung thee asleep, his loving breast thy pillow;/ Many a story hath he told to thee,/ And bid thee bear his pretty tales when he was dead and gone. *Marcus* How many thousand times hath these poor lips,/ When they were living, warm'd themselves on thine!" (5, iii). This is one of the few passages which can read as referring to Shakespeare's own son; another such passage occurs in *The Winter's Tale* (1, ii), where Leontes and Polixenes compare their feelings for their sons: "*Leontes* . . . Are you so fond of your young Prince, as we/ Doe seeme to be of ours? *Polixenes* If at home (Sir)/ He's all my Exercise, my Mirth, my Matter;/ Now my sworne Friend, and then mine Enemy;/ My Parasite, my Souldier: States-man; all:/ He makes a Julyes day, short as December,/ And with his varying child-nesse cures in me/ Thoughts, that would thick my blood."

CHAPTER 8: THE DEER POACHING TRADITION

1 See *The Merry Wives Of Windsor*, lines 1835-1836; Chambers, *op.cit.*, p.264.
2 Chambers, *op.cit.*, p.257
3 *Ibid*, p.265
4 *Ibid*, pp 289, 290
5 *Ibid*, p.293
6 *Ibid*, p.296

7 *Ibid*, p.297
8 *Ibid*, p.301
9 Alice Fairfax-Lucy, *Charlecote And The Lucys* (1958), p.279
10 C. Holte Bracebridge, *Shakespeare No Deerstealer* (1862)
11 J.O.Haliwell-Phillips, *Observations on The Charlecote Traditions* (1887), p.23
12 Chambers, *op.cit.*, p.299
13 Halliday, *op.cit.*, p.291

CHAPTER 9: SIR THOMAS LUCY'S DEER PARKS

1 Jane Croom, *The Medieval Deer Parks Of Warwickshire* (BA Dissertation, Birmingham University 1983)
2 *Ibid;* M.W. Beresford, "The Deserted Medieval Villages In Warwickshire", *Transactions Of The Birmingham Archaelogical Society*, Vol.66 (1950), pp 54, 100
3 Edgar Fripp, *Shakespeare's Haunts Near Stratford* (1929), p.123; *Inq.P.M. II, Vol.43, 50, Trin. Term. 17 Hen VIII, C42/43/50*, in the Public Record Office (afterwards, cited as the P.R.O.)
4 William Dugdale, *The Antiquities Of Warwickshire*, ii, p.670; *Letters & Papers (Foreign & Domestic), Vol.1, Part 1 (1509), 604/22; Del.Weston, 14 Oct., 2 Hen.VIII (1510); Esch. Ing. 17 Hen.8., E150/1130/1* P.R.O. Quoted in Halliwell-Phillips, *Observations On The Charlecote Traditions*, pp, 24, 47, 48
5 Quoted in Fripp, *Shakespeare's Haunts*, pp 123. 124
6 *V.C.H. Of Warwickshire*, Vol.3, p.103
7 *Lucy Fine, Hil. 36 Eliz.*, P.R.O., quoted in Halliwell-Phillips, *Observations On The Charlecote Traditions*, p.25. See also *Calendar Of Patent Rolls, 1548-1549*, p.255
8 Quoted in Fripp, *Shakespeare's Haunts*, p.125; *Patent Roll, 16 James I, ii, 13*, P.R.O.
9 The original is in Charlecote House, and there is a transcript in the Stratford Birthplace Records Office.
10 *E 150/1151 m4, Warwick Inq. taken 23 Sept. 5. Edw.VI, 1551*, P.R.O.; *V.C.H. of Warwickshire*, Vol. 3, p.119
11 *V.C.H. Of Warwickshire*, Vol.3, p.103; *C66/914 m14, Patent Roll 3 & 4 Phillip & Mary, Part 9, 1557*, P.R.O.

12 *V.C.H. Of Warwickshire*, Vol.3, p.102
13 *Ibid, p.103*
14 *C 66/914 m14*, P.R.O.
15 *Wards 7/26/95 and C 142/263,7 (i)*, P.R.O.
16 *Calendar Of Patent Rolls, Edw.VI, Vol.2, 1548-1549*, p.255.
17 *V.C.H. Of Warwickshire*, Vol.3, p.102
18 "An Acte concerninge certyne assurances of Sir Thomas Lucie and others", *27. Eliz.I, No.39*
19 See James Fish, "The Survey Book Of The Manours Of Charlecot & Hunscot With Part Of The Manours Of Hampton-Lucy, Hatton, & Fullbrook In The County Of Warwick All Being The Lands Of The Worshipfull Tho. Lucy Esq" (1736), in the Warwickshire C.R.O., *LS/1036*
20 *V.C.H. Of Warwickshire*, Vol. 2, pp 291, 292
21 *Ibid*, Vol.3, p.91
22 *Letters And Papers (Foreign & Domestic), Hen. VIII, Vol.1, Part 1 (1509), 604 (Grants),22*, P.R.O.
23 *Patent Roll 1 Mary, Part 9 (1553-1554), E 66/872 m25*, P.R.O.
24 *Letters And Papers Foreign And Domestic, Hen.VIII, Vol.7*, p.292., P.R.O.
25 Lucy Toulmin,(Ed) *The Itinerary Of John Leland*, Vol.2 (1964), p.48
26 *V.C.H. Of Warwickshire*, Vol.3, p.93
27 *Harleian MS 607, f.128*, British Library
28 *V.C.H. Of Warwickshire*, Vol.3, p.93
29 *Calendar Of Patent Rolls, 1557-1558*, p.174
30 *Dictionary Of National Biography*, Vol.6, p.791
31 *Calendar Of Patent Rolls, 1569-1572*, p.194
32 *LR 1/135 (Vol.7),f.100 d (1573)*, P.R.O.
33 *SC6 Eliz./2308/2309/2310 (Warwickshire)*, P.R.O.
34 *Calendar Of State Papers, Dom.Ser.,Addenda 1566-1579*, p.509
35 *C66/1107*, P.R.O. See also *Calendar Of Patent Rolls, 1569-1572*, p.46
36 *John Kempson's Survey Of Northbrook Farm, 1813*, in the Warwickshire County Record Office; see also the Ordnance Survey map of Fulbrook parish.
37 See *SC6.Eliz.I.2308*, P.R.O. for a reference to this inquiry.
38 *V.C.H. Of Warwickshire*, Vol.3, p.92
39 *Calendar Of State Papers, Domestic, 1581-1590*, p.632
40 Edgar Fripp, *Shakespeare's Haunts Near Stratford* (1929), pp 116, 117
41 *Calendar Of Patent Rolls, 1575-1578*, p.449

42 *V.C.H. Of Warwickshire,*, Vol.3, p.250
43 In 1595, Adrian Quiney brought an action against Philip Green, Henry Rogers and John Shakespeare for a debt of £5. See Lewis, *op.cit.*, p.68
44 Fripp, *op.cit.*, pp 116, 117
45 Schoenbaum *op.cit.*, p.107
46 *35. Eliz.c.5*
47 *SP 38/8, Warrants 26 September 1607*, P.R.O.
48 *Calendar Of State Papers, Domestic 1603-10*, p.371
49 *Harleian MS 607, f.128*, British Libary
50 *SC6. Eliz.I.2308* and *LR 1/135 (Vol.7), f100d (1573)*, P.R.O.

CHAPTER 10: THE DEER PARK AND CONY WARREN AT CHARLECOTE

1 See *The Sheldon Tapestry Maps* (Warwick Museum Publications); E.A.B.Barnard & A.J.B.Wace, *The Sheldon Tapestry Weavers And Their Work* (1928)
2 John Humpherys, *Elizabethan Sheldon Tapestries* (1929), p.16
3 *L6/254*, Warwickshire C.R.O.
4 C.Holte Bracbridge, *Shakespeare No Deerstealer* (1862), pp 6, 7
5 Fripp, *Shakespeare Haunts op.cit.*, p.124
6 Croom, *op.cit.*, p.12
7 *Ibid*, p.20
8 *Ibid*, p.34
9 H.V.Thompson and A.N.Worden, *The Rabbit* (1956), p.187
10 *Calendar Of State Papers, Addenda 1566-1579*, p.289
11 *L6/191*, Warwickshire C.R.O.
12 *L6/193*, Warwickshire C.R.O.
13 *5.Eliz.I, c.21*
14 *32.Henry VIII, c.11*
15 Quoted in J.O.Halliwell-Phillips, *Observations On The Charlecote Tradition* (1887), pp 15, 16
16 *Ibid*, p.16
17 *Ibid*, p.12

CHAPTER 11: THE WILD YOUTH

1 *The Winter's Tale*, 1501-1507
2 *Cymbeline*, 2834-2842
3 *1, Henry VI*, 1996; *3, Henry VI*, 2363
4 *3, Henry VI*, 1398-1405
5 *Love's Labour's Lost*, 983-984
6 *As You Like It*, 638-650
7 *Much Ado About Nothing*, 619
8 *Coriolanus*, 2870-2871
9 *3, Henry VI*, 523-524
10 *The Merry Wives Of Windsor*, 422-425
11 *Love's Labour's Lost*, 1214-1226
12 *Julius Caesar*, 1426-1432
13 *As You Like It*, 663-665
14 *Titus Andronicus*, 1228-1230
15 *Ibid*, 642-655
16 *Venus And Adonis*
17 *Twelth Night*, 24-28
18 *Venus And Adonis*
19 *Hamlet*, 913-915
20 *Love's Labour's Lost*, 1565
21 *Ibid*, 1963-1964
22 *All's Well That Ends Well*, 2703-2705
23 *Measure For Measure*, 294-295 & 309-310
24 *Timon Of Athens*, 1883-1886
25 Halliday, *op.cit.*, p.443
26 Ralph Houlbroke, "The Making Of Marriage In Mid-Tudor England: Evidence From The Records Of Matrimonial Contract Legislation", *Journal Of Family History*, Vol.10 (1985), pp 339-351
27 J.M.Martin, *Marriage And Population Change In Tudor And Stuart Warwickshire* (1973. Manuscript thesis in the Warwickshire C.R.O.), p.36
28 *Ibid*, p.25
29 Skipp, *op.cit.*, p.14
30 *The Tempest*, 1666-1675
31 *Ibid*, 2269-2270
32 *Ibid*, 494-498

33 *Hamlet*, 3252-3255 & 3263-3266
34 *Love's Labour's Lost*, 2277-2278
35 *Twelth Night*, 2318-2322
36 *Much Ado About Nothing*, 1704-1708
37 *As You Like It*, 1504-1506
38 Chambers, *op.cit.*, p.253
39 *A Midsummer's Night's Dream*, 2186-2192
40 *Henry V*, 3168-3169
41 *The Taming Of The Shrew*, 2663-2665
42 *As You Like It*, 2055-2056
43 *All's Well That Ends Well*, 2041-2043
44 *The Comedy Of Errors*, 1516-1549
45 *Ibid*, 620 & 770-775
46 *Ibid*, 789-809
47 *Othello*, 3066-3076
48 *Love's Labour's Lost*, 1596 & 1603-1604
49 *Romeo And Juliet*, 1109-1110
50 *As You Like It*, 1839-1840
51 *A Midsummer's Night's Dream*, 584-590
52 *King Lear*, 2467-2471
53 See for example *Cymberline*, 5, v and *Twelth Night*, 5, i
54 *The Comedy Of Errors*, 364-381
55 *All's Well That Ends Well*, 1199-1200
56 *Ibid*, 944-45

CHAPTER 12: BANISHMENT AND EXILE

1 *King Lear*, 1913-1914
2 *Ibid*, 696-698
3 *Ibid*, 2, ii (Alexander Edition)
4 *All's Well That Ends Well*, 874-877
5 *Ibid*, 1164-1165
6 *The Winter's Tale*, 1757-1758
7 *Anthony And Cleopatra*, 2265, 2273-2278, 2309-2313
8 *Romeo And Juliet*, 304-305
9 *All's Well That Ends Well*, 2290-2292
10 *Love's Labour's Lost*, 2636-2637

11 *A Midsummer's Night's Dream*, 172-173
12 *Hamlet*, 1570-1571
13 *King Lear*, 2595-2606
14 *Romeo And Juliet*, 1815-1826
15 *King Lear*, 993-995 & 1018-1921
16 *Ibid*, 1809-1810 & 1698-1706
17 *Coriolanus*, 3317, 3373-3374, 3383-3385, 3394
18 *Ibid*, 2659-2692
19 *Ibid*, pp 285, 286
20 *Romeo And Juliet*, 2798-2802
21 *As You Like It*, 10-11
22 *The Taming Of The Shrew*, 616-618

CHAPTER 13: THE RISE OF WILLIAM SHAKESPEARE

1 Chambers, *William Shakespeare*, Vol.2, pp 252, 253
2 Quoted in S.Schoenbaum, *Shakespeare's Lives* (1970), pp 122, 123
3 Chambers, *op.cit.*, p.259
4 *Ibid*, p.254
5 *Ibid*, pp 264, 265
6 *The Merchant Of Venice*, 787-790
7 *Cymbeline*, 3176-3182
8 Fripp, *Master Richard Quyney*, p.177
9 Phelps-Brown & Hopkins, *op.cit.*, p.189
10 Quoted in Skipp, *op.cit.*, p.48
11 Thirsk, *op.cit.*, p.857
12 Fripp, *op.cit.*, p.103
13 Lewis, *op.cit.*, p.284
14 *Ibid*, p.285
15 *Ibid*, p.227
16 *Ibid*, pp 281-283
17 Quoted in Ann Hughes, *Politics, Society And Civil War In Warwickshire 1620-1660* (1987), p.83
18 Halliday, *op.cit.*, p.400
19 *Julius Caesar*, 638-643
20 *Coriolanus*, 80-85 & 17-26
21 See Annabel Patterson, *Shakespeare And The Popular Voice* (1989)

22 Brian Manning, *Village Revolts, Social Protest And Popular Disturbances In England, 1509-1640* (1988), p.204
23 *Timon Of Athens*, 1518-1531
24 *Troilus And Cressida*, 560-583

CHAPTER 14: THE END OF EXILE

1 See Lawrence Stone, "Interpersonal Violence In English Society 1300-1980", *Past And Present*, Vol.101 (1983), pp 22-33; Martin Daly and Margo Wilson, *Homicide* (1988), p.276; Razzell, *op.cit.*, pp vii-xxi
2 J.B.Given, *Society And Homicide In Thirteenth Century England* (1977). Alan Macfarlane has argued that individualism was not confined to the towns, but was a general characteristic of English society at this time; his thesis is however controversial and would have to be qualified by the generally accepted fact that the open field system involved a major degree of communalism. See Alan Macfarlane, *The Origins Of English Individualism* (1978)
3 Emile Durkheim, *Suicide: A Study In Sociology* (1952), pp 278-282
4 J.A.Sharpe, *Crime In Early Modern England: 1550-1750* (1984), pp 54-56
5 Manning, *op.cit.*, p.187
6 John Graunt, *Natural And Political Observations Made Upon The Bills Of Mortaility* (1662), p.74 In order to calculate these rates, I have used the population figures for London given in Finlay, *op.cit.* Finlay has concluded that the London bills of mortality were more reliable than hitherto thought. However, it should be noted that London's suicide rate was surprisingly low at this time; for example, the rate for Kent during the period 1561-1600 was 10.0 per 100,000, although this may have been higher than elsewhere because of its proximity to London. See Michael Zell, "Suicide In Pre-Industrial England", *Social History*, Vol.11 (1986), p.309.
7 See Razzell, *op.cit.*, p.xxxii; Zell, *op.cit.*
8 Graunt, *op.cit.*, p.22
9 Keith Wrightson, *English Society: 1580-1680* (1982), pp 190, 194
10 Razzell in Gough, *op.cit.*, pp xiv, xv
11 See Schoenbaum, *op.cit.*, pp 233, 234, 238

12 Chambers, *William Shakespeare*, Vol.2, p.252
13 *Ibid*, pp 250, 268, 286, 291
14 *The Tempest*, 2005-2008
15 *The Winter's Tale*, 2727-2732
16 *Ibid*, 3306-3317
17 Chambers, *op.cit.*, pp 268, 269
18 *Ibid*, p.250
19 *The Tempest*, 1209-1210
20 *Ibid*, 2292-2294
21 *Ibid*, 1445-1447
22 *As You Like It*, 618-623. I have modernized this passage appropriate to the context.

INDEX

(This index makes no reference to either William or John Shakespeare)